The Light Point

A TESTIMONY OF OVERCOMING INSECURITY,
FINDING IDENTITY, AND DISCOVERING
INTIMACY WITH CHRIST

*Dear Madison,
I truly value your
friendship and
support. Thank
you for joining
me in the
light. I love
you*

SIJI DELEAWE

This book is dedicated to my parents, David and Agnes Deleawe. Thank you for loving me like God and showing me what it looks like to live in the light.

"For you were once darkness, but now you are light in the Lord. Live as children of light (for the fruit of the light consists in all goodness, righteousness and truth)...."

Ephesians 5:8-9 (NIV)

Contents

Preface

Why I'm afraid to write this book:

1. I am afraid that my loved ones will read this radically transparent book and know too much about what I struggled with sexually if I am as honest as God is calling me to be. I'm scared that their opinions of me will change. They may not love me less, but I'm afraid that they will love me differently. I've never before been forced to hold up the opinions of those closest to me against the opinion of God. I've never had to confront the fact that I may desire their approval more than His. I'm not sure if they will understand why I am being this open, or if

they will see that disobedience isn't an option for me. I'm afraid that once I shatter their perceptions of my innocence, they will desperately desire to see me as I was, only to find that the girl who existed in their minds once before is gone forever.

2. I am not sure my sin is "relatable" enough. Some people have done much more, and some people have done much less. I'm scared that in my truth, some will feel condemned and others will feel indifferent.

3. I am afraid that I will be misinterpreted or misunderstood. I am afraid that my words will not be clear enough and that my testimony will not be bold enough. I don't want anyone to misconstrue my reasons for writing this book. I'm afraid that people won't realize that this book is not really about me at all. I'm afraid that they'll focus so much on why I wrote the book that they'll miss the point—Jesus.

When God first instructed me to write this book, I wrote this list instead. I allowed these fears to define my response. I straight up told God, "No." I thought He was asking too much of me, so I refused. However, in His patient kindness and loving mercy, God never gave up on me. Even when I selfishly ran away from not only what He called me to do but who He called me to be, He waited for me. I was Jonah, called to a lost people, but I was so concerned with my comfort that I tried to escape my destiny. I desperately tried to resist God's calling, but I knew I couldn't, so I attempted to talk myself out of obedience by grounding myself in fear. I found myself in the belly of the whale of despair. Fear wasn't the enemy; it was simply used by the enemy to draw me away from my purpose.

Looking back, I realized that every single one of the fears I listed was based on what others would think of me. However, I had to stop and ask myself, *What will God think of me? Why aren't I more afraid of breaking God's heart when I profess to serve Him with my mouth but refuse to answer His call with my actions? Why am I more afraid of disappointment than disobedience?*

There are scary, uncomfortable realities I might have to face by publishing this book, but they are completely hypothetical. The enemy isn't a mind-reader. He simply makes inferences from what I say and the cycles of self-sabotage he's seen me fall into in the past. For a moment, the devil was able to take my fears and make them feel huge and real and tangible. They moved out of the realm of my thoughts and into a reality I had to confront before they could cripple me. That tricky devil presented all these fears to me as legitimate. The truth is, although I have well-thought-out concerns, they aren't mine to be concerned about. God knows what can and will go wrong.

Since He made me, God also knew I would fixate on the reasons why I shouldn't write this book. So almost immediately after I received the instructions to write it, and after I put my fears on paper, God spoke very clearly and said, "Just write." I was not to concern myself with anything else. Not what other people or even my parents might think, not how unqualified I was in both life experience and practical knowledge, not who might read it or decide that reading it wasn't worth their time, none of that. He said to just write. So, of course, I began to do everything other than write. I can see how it all worked out for good now. The further I tried to run away, the more consuming the calling became. It was all I could see, all I could think about. Every social media post, every song, and every conversation all led back to what God told me to do and what I very clearly wasn't doing.

Preface

Every time I tried to ignore the call, I heard a voice say, "Just write." It took me several painful months. I felt as unqualified as Moses standing in front of a burning bush, concerned about a speech impediment when God was calling him to freedom. Eventually, I could no longer disobey the Holy Spirit. God needs this story to go out into the world and He wants to use me as the vessel to send it.

However, looking back on my journey, I still had so many fears when it came to writing this book. Some were legitimate and some were ridiculous. The devil tried to use those fears to trap me in the bondage of shame and self-doubt, but of course, God already knew I would be victorious. He just needed me to believe victory could look different than I expected.

The strange thing is that God didn't take away my fears in order to get me to write this book. They were there every day, constantly in the back of my mind. Some days, they physically paralyzed me and made it impossible for me to write a word. I thought God was supposed to bring me to a place of total peace and calm about the situation and then I'd be able to write my story without any fear. But because He is God—the God of David, Gideon, and Peter—He is able to use those of us who are still afraid. Our fears may never disappear; instead, they might simply be placed in proper perspective. The book you're reading right now wasn't written because I am fearless. It was written because God gave me the ability to see my fears in the light and realize they were not powerful enough to stop the purpose of God for my life.

As I journaled in preparation for this challenge of a lifetime, God continued to say, "Just write." He clearly spoke to my spirit and told me, "Just write, and I will do the rest. I won't give you more than you can handle. I won't expose you until your eyes are ready to adjust to the light. Constantly recalibrate your heart and study the Word to be shown approved. Get in the Word, and let it transform you. Peace, be still. I am with you. I will never leave you nor forsake you. My perfect love casts out all fear. Just write."

God showed me that our fears are just like shifting shadows in dimly-lit rooms. They appear so much bigger than they are. When they're projected against the walls of our insecurities, our fears seem to be inescapable, all-consuming. They seem to loom larger than our faith. Sometimes when you're looking at a shadow, it appears frightening because you can't see the object that cast it. All God did was turn me around and help me see my fear for what it really was. In comparison to what God called me to do, my fear was small. I was able to pick that fear up and stare it in the face. I examined it from every side. I inspected it, turned it inside out and upside down, and I was able to recognize that it was powerless. I didn't render it powerless. God didn't even render it powerless. It simply became apparent that it had been powerless all along. Although the fear was still there, God gave me the grace to turn on the lights. I saw that I didn't have to be bound by my fear. So, with my mustard-seed faith in one hand and my story in the other, I wrote anyway.

I faced my fears head-on every day as I wrote this book, because where I come from, I've never seen anybody be quite this transparent. I don't have a bad background. In fact, my upbringing was so good, so right, and so Godly that it terrified me to let the world know I'd fallen short of that standard. I was raised with so much intentional effort to present me with the light of goodness that I thought people would be confused and wonder how I could have dealt with all I discuss in this book. As I wrote, I could clearly picture the faces of those who grew up around me and never knew, never even suspected what I was going though. I was sure they would wonder what could've gone wrong. I was scared to write this book because I understood their questions. I wanted to know the same thing. What went wrong?

As I continued to write, the light of God's presence revealed so much about who I was and who He called me to be. I became intimately acquainted with my flaws and deficiencies in the year I wrote this book. As badly as I wanted to be David, I felt like Saul—knowing I could never outrun God but still trying to run faster than Him anyway. It was a process that allowed me to clearly see my imperfections and realize how badly I needed to trust God. I had to learn how to run toward God instead of away from Him, even when things got hard. I desperately wanted to hold on to my Savior and my fears at the same time, but there simply wasn't room for both of them. God never left my side, but I would have to release my fears to really cling to Him in the way that I needed to if I was going to do what He asked of me.

It sounds strange, but in some ways, I liked my fears. I felt like they kept me grounded in a reality where I had some semblance of control over my future. I held my fears close like a warm blanket on a rainy day. I thought I had a hold on them, but they really had a hold on me.

I was well on my way to allowing my fear to kill my destiny and suffocate my testimony before I even had the chance to impact the lives God called me to touch. I was well on my way to being silenced before I even had a chance to speak, to being bound before I ever had a chance to be free, and to planting roots in the dark before I even had the opportunity to grow in the light. But God.

God, being God, reached down into my little train of fear and snatched me off the tracks. He sent me word after word, confirmation after confirmation, encouragement after encouragement. I was looking for something to stand on, and the God who saw my heart did not forsake me. He said:

"I am with you, *just write.*"

"Let me handle all the details, *just write.*"

"This is bigger than you, *just write.*"

"I use the foolish things of the world to confuse the wise, *just write.*"

"All things work together for good, *just write.*"

And so I did.

It was an imperfect process. Some days I wrote ten pages and then for two weeks I wouldn't write a single word. I wanted to feel like writing; I didn't want to feel like God was trying to give me a divine research project. But I had to submit my feelings to my faith and just write.

As I began to believe more and more that God is who He says He is and that He really spoke a word over my life, my writing grew in confidence and consistency. I wasn't just writing to write; I was quite literally writing my way into purpose. Writing became that thing I could do all day for free. It became the thing that felt more like joy than work.

Some days, I still had to remain consistent through sheer discipline, but God gave me grace for the process.

Things changed when I began to feel honored and humbled that God had chosen me despite what it might cost me. The more I sought Him, the more I realized that a book which started off with me at the center was really supposed to have God at the center. I can't get very far talking about myself, but the God of the universe? Now that's a life-changing subject.

This book exists because what the enemy planned for evil God turned around and used for my good. This book was written according to His will and according to His timeline. It was developed through a process that God knew would change me forever, and so like Paul, by the grace of God, I boast in my weaknesses. I am able to be vulnerable about my mistakes so that you may see them and testify of the goodness of God.

My heart's desire, in the depth of my soul, is that when you read this book, you will not just see me. This book holds my unique experience, but it's about so much more than me. This is *The Light Point*, and it should point you to Jesus. For all who read to see Christ, know Christ, and love Christ—that is the sole purpose and mission of this book. It is a culmination of my brokenness, my pain, my redemption, my healing, and the joy of God's salvation.

However, if I can say this so boldly, this book was not written by me. Only the Holy Spirit could've done this work. Only the Christ in me could have been brave enough to say what needed to be said. I am simply a vessel. I'm not saying this out of false humility, I'm saying this because it is true. For months, I tried to run away from the work God was trying to do. For months, He waited on me patiently until I sat down and let Him move. I'm saying this because I know myself and I know what I'm capable of, but I also know that this book will be a blessing to you, and that is something only God is capable of. So please, if you read this, read it searching for God. I believe that He will reveal Himself to you in such a way that your life will never ever be the same.

The first person whose life was changed by this book was me. In writing it, I found the light. My hope is that it will do the same for you. I pray that this book will inspire you to share your story so that you too can live free from fear and shame. I pray that these pages will illuminate the Truth of the Gospel. I pray that the words you read point you to Christ. So come, let us walk boldly and bravely into the light.

Preface

- *One* -

THE ORIGINS

It is dark here. There is pain that chokes the breath out of her lungs
Stealing the air that would have carried words into the world
She is unliving, less than breath,
Breathless
Fire surrounds her
Singeing everything that she once held so closely

I think the first time I was exposed to anything
sexual was with other church kids. Some of the
older teens were watching us while our parents
were at our church's annual Couples Love Banquet. The
details are fuzzy, but I remember one of the older teenage
boys pulling out his penis and flashing everyone. He ran

around the room and chased people. Some of the other kids kept turning off the lights, and we all screamed because it was pretty late. It was all very silly. I just remember realizing that I'd never seen that part of a boy's body before and never telling any adult in my life what happened in that room or even mentioning it outside of that day. I truly thought it was insignificant and I didn't even remember it until recently. But it was a seed that was planted in my subconscious, through no fault of my own, and it led to a curiosity about boys and their bodies. I was seven.

I don't remember learning about sex—I don't remember not knowing how things worked. I got my period in fifth grade when I was ten, almost eleven, and my mom gave me a book called *My Body and Me*. It was pink and had laughing girls on the cover. I always wondered what they found so funny; this sexuality thing seemed like pretty serious business to me. The first thing I was told when I got my period was that I could now get pregnant. I already knew this, of course, but I guess the reminder was nice. The book included diagrams that showed how my body would evolve and how the sexual parts of men and women worked. I flipped through it, forgetting all the scientific labels as soon as I turned the page and ignoring the stuff that I didn't understand. Asking questions was out of the question, so I put the book in my drawer and never looked at it again.

No one ever told me I couldn't talk about sex, but no one ever told me I could, either. Therefore, I was left to do what I saw others do around me—which, for the most part, was to remain silent on the topic. It either wasn't important enough to discuss or it was so serious that it became taboo. Whatever it was, I knew innately never to bring it up. I don't blame the adults around me at all. They simply did what they knew; however, their choice of silence became an unspoken obligation that I felt the burden to bear as well. Soon, that silence would become so loud that it would threaten to suffocate me under its weight. But at that moment, at ten years old, it simply felt comfortable.

...

Growing up, I'd always been an avid reader. I used to check out books from the library and read all day, for hours and hours. I developed the habit because, from elementary school all the way up through high school, my siblings and I weren't allowed to watch TV on the weekdays. We didn't have TVs in our rooms, and as the youngest sibling, I had no right to the remote, so reading was the more exciting option for me. I had a huge imagination as a child and was almost perpetually bored, so books became my home. They were an escape into a far more interesting reality. Then, when I was about eleven years old, we moved to a new house where I finally got my own room and my own computer.

Out of the infinite things I could have used the Internet for, I found a way to use it to read more. There was a website where I could read free books posted by both amateur and experienced writers. This was right before the fan-fiction era, so these stories weren't based on celebrities or anything. The website was filled with people who liked to write, so they posted full-length works, chapter by chapter, and amassed large followings of young readers. Some of these stories were hundreds of pages long. I was reading about worlds that were entirely fictional and, like most young, impressionable girls, I soon became obsessed. At a time when I had little access to the library and no money to buy books, this website became my world. My family had moved across town to a sleepy neighborhood where I didn't know anyone. I was a pretty lonely kid who found it hard to make friends in a new environment. The online reading site became a safe space where I could lose myself in stories.

I began using the website innocently enough, but then I accidently stumbled onto some books that were really raunchy and sexually explicit. They were completely inappropriate for an eleven-year-old, but the beauty and terror of the Internet is that it is open to all—no matter how young and impressionable you are. Unsurprisingly, these sexual books were the most popular stories on the website—it wasn't even close. I was so young and sheltered that I never for a moment connected the popularity of these books to their sexually explicit nature. I simply thought the writing was excellent. And just like that, I was hooked. I used to read these sexually explicit novels for hours a day. At the time, the stories didn't seem that crude because they were written as love stories about people in high school or college.

At that age, I found school generally boring and unengaging, so reading these stories became the highlight of my days living in my South Dallas suburb. I was that kid who was notorious for racking up library fines because I would hold on to the books I borrowed long after they were due. Therefore, the convenience of this new, free way to read was unbelievably appealing to me. I would spend hours locked inside my room reading these books eagerly, consuming the high-drama love stories. I believe that my love for reading is a gift from God, but during this time, the enemy took that lovely gift and perverted it, making my obsession with these books grow in an unhealthy way.

The stories were great, but the real attraction was the way they made me feel. To put it mildly, the feeling was arousal, something I didn't even have the word for at the time. I couldn't really explain why I felt pleasure but guilt at the same time. However, I somehow knew not to tell anyone. I put on silence like a protective shield against my confusion. I didn't have to deal with that which was only a reality in my mind. I knew my voice was powerful. Using it might compel me to confront my shame, so I chose to be quiet. More than just comfortable, silence became safe.

As I continued to read, I reached a point where I couldn't read a book unless it gave me that aroused feeling. I never told another soul about this obsession. It didn't feel all the way wrong, but it didn't feel right, either. I was so eager for the pleasure these stories brought me that I would read them slowly, knowing that when I was done the feeling would fade and I would have to wait for a new fix in the next chapter.

I was raised in a really strict Christian household, but my upbringing didn't cause me to initially categorize these books as bad or nasty because they didn't seem to be solely focused on sex. In my mind, they were love stories. Even at that age, I was enthralled by the idea of romance and relationships. I had inherited a culture of silence around the concept of sex, but that didn't stop me from being curious.

Just because those questions didn't come out of my mouth didn't mean they weren't in my mind. Curiosity isn't something that just disappears. Children, and even adults, don't simply settle for blank space when there are no answers to our questions. There is always something that steps in to quell our curiosity in the absence of objective Truth. The trick is to define where that something comes from, because lies are abundant but the Truth is very specific.

The ideas presented in these books placed me in the dangerous world of one who believes lies as truths. When graphic descriptions of sex and sexual acts came up, I didn't feel awkward about continuing to read because I fully bought into the stories. I could paint these brilliantly realistic pictures of what I was reading in my mind. They were so detailed that sometimes they took lives of their own and became mixed up in the space that holds memories and dreams. However, once again, the devil perverted this perfectly creative trait in a toxic way. I truly believed that what was described in these novels was love. I thought that was how relationships worked. I had no truth to compare them to. I was extremely susceptible and naive at the time, and reading these stories ensured that my first understanding of romantic love was warped and perverted.

First, the women in these stories always had something terrible happening to them. They were always either sick, stuck in abusive households, or faced bullying at school. It therefore set the stage for the men to always be the heroes. It's one of the most common tropes in literature, but it can be a dangerous concept for a young, impressionable mind. In these books, a man's love was not just this nice thing that he offered a woman. It was necessary. It saved her from some terrible, lonely fate. I'm so far out of that mindset now that it's a little difficult to remember exactly what I was thinking when reading these stories, but I know I was a bright kid. I knew it wasn't real and that these were just stories that were highly exaggerated for dramatic benefit. But the underlying ideas still seeped into my mind and unintentionally defined the way I looked at the world.

I remember reading one book where this girl was abducted by a vampire and used as a sex slave. Yeah, it got really twisted and kinky and every sexual act was described in graphic detail, but I kept reading anyway. I was way too young to be consuming those things now that I look back at it, but when you're a kid you never feel as young as you are. I couldn't have known the danger I was in. After all, if I was reading like my parents wanted me to, then how bad could it be? I did think it was a bit strange that I'd get

aroused when I read certain scenes, but it felt good, so I chalked it up to good writing and kept it pushing.

It got to a point where I kept searching for that feeling when reading and started caring less about the actual content of the writing. I don't know when I stopped really feeling excited by normal books. I only wanted to read the ones where the girl had gone through some type of trauma and her relationship with this man who swept her off her feet either fixed the issue or made it go away.

Second, a common theme in all of these stories was that they involved the man falling madly in love after one encounter, which seems so ridiculous now. Oftentimes, the male protagonist was actually abusive in some way. Sometimes, he was just using the girl until he suddenly had a change of heart and ended up falling for her. He'd suddenly discover he was madly in love with her because she'd loved him through his abuse. Other times, it was the man who saved her from an abusive situation and he saw her as gorgeous when she couldn't see her own worth. Somehow, she wasn't able to see her beauty unless it was acknowledged by a man. These women had no autonomy; their lives were defined by someone else's lust.

I suppose my sexual sin began when I started to allow these lustful and perverse desires from the books I read to take root in my heart. What started off as simply trying to read easily accessible content eventually led to me thinking perverted thoughts and fantasizing about the scenes in these novels even when I wasn't reading. It felt wrong, but I couldn't seem to stop, so I found myself drowning in shame. The problem was that instead of just feeling ashamed of my thoughts, I began to feel ashamed of myself. I didn't know how to differentiate between hating what I was doing and hating who I was.

I think it's important to recognize that this wasn't just wrong "because God said so," although that reason would be enough. It was also wrong because those thoughts were deceptive. These books painted false realities of relationships, love, sex, and intimacy. They got into my impressionable mind and disguised themselves as truth before the real Truth could take root. What started off as innocent entertainment became a shameful addiction over time because I knew I couldn't just stop reading. I knew the words were not staying safely confined in the realm of fiction. I knew that, like a cunning snake, they were making their way into my reality and subtly reshaping my desires, expectations, and perceptions of others and myself.

For a while, the thoughts were just thoughts. I was stimulated and aroused by what I was reading, but nothing more than that. However, the Bible says in Proverbs 4:23 (ESV), "Keep your heart with all vigilance, for from it flow the springs of life." Soon, what was in my heart would begin to manifest destructively in my life.

Even before I ever acted on those thoughts, I had a lot of unaddressed guilt. In hindsight, I know the guilt came from the shame of knowing that something was wrong. I couldn't run up to my parents and tell them about what I was reading. In fact, I didn't talk to anyone about the details of it. I just kept it to myself. When I first started reading these sexualized books as a child, I just felt kind of embarrassed. But as I grew older, that feeling solidified itself in my heart as shame. It was my little secret that no one needed to know because it didn't match up with who I presented myself to be. I convinced myself that it wasn't that deep. Much later, I realized that if it wasn't that deep, I would not be so anxious and afraid of what people would think if I talked about it.

I think it's also important to acknowledge that no one taught me to be guilty or ashamed about those desires. Yes, I grew up in a Christian household that said, "No sex before marriage," but that was the extent of my knowledge. Since I never told anyone in my family or church what I was doing or feeling, they couldn't have been the ones to make me feel like it was bad or wrong. And every other influence in my life socialized me to believe that sexual expression was good. But even at that tender age, I had an intrinsic sense of right and wrong, and I knew that I was wrong.

Like so many young girls, my early ideas of love, lust, validation, pain, beauty, and acceptance were all muddled together in a very toxic and deceptive way through my reading. I spent hours learning that my worth was tied to male affection. This constant confusion and disinformation imperceptibly altered the truth and distorted the way my world was shaped. The cracks were small, but they were there. The seeds of deception went deep because they found no resistance when it came time for them to plant themselves in the soil of my heart. A lie is only revealed as such when it is held beside some truth. Darkness is only revealed as such when we've had an encounter with the light.

During this time in my adolescence, there were no opposing truths I could hold up in comparison. There was nothing to prevent me from believing that the distorted image I had in front of me was anything different from the original design. I had no reference point. I did not understand that the God of my salvation was also the God of my sexuality. My faith was not understood as a holistic thing that changed my entire life. After all, I'd been a Christian since before I could remember. I'd said the prayer of salvation when I was five, and then again at seven, and then one more time at ten during church camp. There was no me before the knowledge of Christ, or so I thought. Because I thought I already had all of God, I never went looking for more of Him, and I never imagined He might care about me reading sexually explicit books online or the ways those books impacted my thoughts and desires.

The Origins

- Two -

NOT QUITE FREE

She bangs against the cage that
They used to bury her alive
She is suffocating
Arms shaking
Heart palpitating
Breath fading
Her instincts kick in and
She finds the strength for one last struggle

ventually, reading was not enough. I wanted to try some of the things I had read. I didn't want to wait for a specific chapter or scene to make me feel aroused; I wanted to control that feeling. However, because there was still that sense of shame attached to these feelings of arousal, I only explored them late at night while in bed and under the covers. I tried to masturbate, but I couldn't seem to get exactly what I desired. So instead, I went back to my vivid imagination and created scenarios in my mind where I was one of the characters in the books I'd read.

Sometimes, I'd make up my own stories, but every time there was a man (or I guess an older boy since I was so young at this time) pleasuring me in some way. I'd arouse myself with these fantasies at night before I went to bed so I could pretend that my very real actions were as fictional as the words I had been reading on a screen. It felt less strange because I was able to escape into a sleepy, almost-subconscious, in-between state that felt kind of like a dream even though I wasn't asleep.

As I did this, the shame grew worse. I'd feel bad before I did it, but the urge was so strong that I would end up doing it anyway—arousing myself—and then go back to immediately feeling guilty afterwards.

I don't even know how many times I promised myself that it was the last time, while feeling confused and disgusted with myself, only to do it the next night or a week later. I would find creative ways to wear clothes to bed in order to live out these truly perverted fantasies in my mind. I was thirteen at this point. I remember succumbing to my desires after resisting for a week or even a month. I remember feeling sick to my stomach and embarrassed that I couldn't control myself. Each time, I would promise myself that it would be the last time, but deep down I knew it wasn't. I didn't think I was addicted at the time. But the reality was I couldn't stop. Like a fiend, I kept going back to get my fix. Even if I stayed away for a couple of weeks, I would always find myself back in that spot, late at night under the covers, with my hands and my imagination.

It got worse when I started talking to boys. They were just long, adolescent, flirty text messages between church kids who didn't have cars and weren't allowed to go on dates, but they were enough to bring that desire to the point where I knew it had too much control over me. I remember crying one night and feeling overwhelmed with shame. I felt guilty and dirty, but I knew that I liked it and wondered how it could feel so good if it was so wrong.

All this time I had the Internet, but I was so paranoid about keeping this secret that I thought I might get caught searching for answers. I had seen my sister get into trouble too many times, so I did everything I could to maintain my persona as "the good daughter." At some point I learned how to delete search histories and then set out trying to figure out exactly what was wrong with me. And do you know what the Internet told me? It told me that masturbation was good! That it was a healthy, normal part of being a young person. So now, not only did I feel wrong, I also felt stupid for feeling so much shame about something that wasn't even a big deal.

I had no idea what to believe. I just knew that these feelings were taking over my life and changing the way I looked at people, including myself. I felt so lost and so guilty all the time. My family was very conservative. So of course, I wasn't going to utter a word of this to any of them. I didn't have any close friends or adults who I could talk to, so I was stuck, trapped, and unable to get help. I couldn't even say my prayers at night because I thought God must think I was filthy. I thought He'd be so disappointed in me for not being able to stop. I promised God I would stop so many times. Then I'd slip up and go right back to my addiction, so I figured He didn't want to hear what I had to say.

I think I must have gone on playing out these sexual fantasies by myself for years before everything came to a head at fourteen years old. I finally broke free of the addiction in a moment of divine intervention. I still can't fully understand what went down that night, and I've never experienced anything quite like it since, but I knew I had reached my breaking point.

My whole family was asleep. I recall lying in bed, fighting the urge to arouse myself. In a memory that feels more like a dream than anything else, I summoned the willpower to get out of bed. I wasn't the most spiritual person at the time, but I knew Jesus and tried to love him. I hated feeling like anything at all had power over me, like I wasn't free to stop. It literally felt like a weight was on me, a shameful secret that made me feel dirty and far from the God I was finally understanding how to love.

I went downstairs and walked around, praying and begging God to break this addiction. That sort of prayer was very out of character for me, and this was the first time I had ever been vulnerable about this urge I felt like I couldn't control. I had asked for forgiveness from this sexual sin before, but I had never asked for deliverance from it. I had never admitted that I felt like it left me feeling broken and unclean, longing for something that was just out of reach. I know the Holy Spirit was helping me pray in that moment because I was saying things I had never said before and wouldn't realize until years later. I walked around my house literally calling out the spirit of sexual perversion and unclean desires from my mind. I kept my voice low so I would not wake anyone up, but I poured out my heart to my Savior. I was silently sobbing, crying out for God to free me from the control of sexual addiction. I didn't know what else to do, so I prayed and prayed for what felt like hours, pleading for God to answer me because I knew I had to get into my bed and go to sleep that night, and I didn't want to wake up with the guilt and shame in the morning.

While I prayed, there was no voice from Heaven or visible sign that I'd been freed. But the image of chains falling off came into my mind and I felt an unfamiliar peace when I stopped praying. I must have exhausted myself because I went to sleep as soon as my head hit the pillow, and from that day forward I never did it again. I still had the desire; God didn't take that away. He just gave me the strength to resist. Looking back, I know the Holy Spirit intervened in my situation before I even really knew who he was, but at the time, I was honestly shocked that God answered my prayer. However, as a young, innocent Christian, I was scared to jeopardize it. So I stopped reading those books altogether and just moved on. At least, I thought I did.

Although I was delivered, I wasn't quite free. I refused to talk about my struggle and I had no idea how to process the mental and emotional toll those years had on me. I shoved it deep down into the box labeled "strange things that happened when I was young" and forgot about it. I think my mind literally blocked out the memory because it was such a traumatic experience for me. Even though I forgot the details for years, the seeds of shame and deception were already planted in the fertile ground of my adolescent heart, and they were growing rapidly into trees of sin that produced all kinds of bad fruit.

By the grace of God, I chopped down those trees when I stopped, but in my haste to move past it, I forgot about the roots of shame, lust, perversion, and impurity that had grown deep down into my heart and mind. By refusing to think about it, pleasure and sexuality were wholly relegated to the realm of sin, leaving no room for the understanding of how God-given desires are good when used in the context that He divinely ordained. So, even though I was delivered from one addiction, I was not freed from the consequences that came later, because I'd only *suppressed* feelings that were meant to be *surrendered*.

. . .

For years, I never told anyone about what I used to do under my sheets at night, not even my best friends. At the time, I would have described the feeling as embarrassment, but now I know the more accurate name for it was shame.

I was ashamed of what I had done, and I didn't fully understand why I had done it or why I found it so hard to stop. In fact, I didn't even understand how I eventually broke free from the addiction. I had no conscious awareness of the Holy Spirit. I just knew that after that night of prayer, I was set free from the action. But unfortunately, I could not escape the impact it had on my mind.

I think I was so relieved it was over that I unintentionally repressed all those memories. The fact that I'd only ever done it at night, in the dark, and that I never spoke about it made it less real for me. To speak to another person about what I'd done would have brought it out of my mind and into another person's reality. It would have given my sin substance and allowed my shameful experience to live on in a mind I had no control over.

Control was big for me. I wanted to control how I was perceived and what other people thought about me. My sexual behavior all those years didn't align with what I had come to know about myself. It was as though I became another person in those moments, someone I didn't recognize and was never forced to face. I figured it wouldn't hurt anyone if I didn't tell anyone; but that's the thing about secrets—they always hurt someone, even if that person is yourself. Secrets build a home for shame, allowing them to settle in and get comfortable in a cocoon of darkness.

As Brené Brown puts it, "Shame hates it when we reach out and tell our story. It hates having words wrapped around it—it can't survive being shared. Shame loves secrecy. When we bury our story, the shame metastasizes."[1]

And that's exactly what I did. I buried this secret part of my story deep down in my memory where no one would be able to find it—not even me. However, that's the funny thing about guilt and shame. They always find a way to show themselves. Because the seeds of my secret were buried deep, the plant of that experience still grew. In fact, the roots of shame were so invasive that they spread and began to affect the outcomes of other areas of my life. Everything I did, unbeknownst to me, had a little bit of shame attached to it. I didn't recognize it because it concealed itself well under perfectionism, performance, and people-pleasing, but it was there. It corrupted the purity of anything else I tried to produce. There was no way I could have known that the shadows of my secrets would impact how I saw myself and others so completely, but looking back, I realize how keeping a secret to try and protect myself really left me exposed and vulnerable.

---

[1] Brown, Brené. *The Gifts of Imperfection*. Simon and Schuster, 2010.

. . .

Growing up, I remember always wanting to be the best at whatever I did. I always had the desire to impress people around me or make adults proud of me. However, when I got to the end of middle school, at the height of my addiction, I became obsessed with being liked, or at least being part of the group of people who seemed to be most liked. It was the typical adolescent story of the new girl who switched schools and just wanted to find her place. Objectively, I was destined for failure before I even started, because I was very different from everyone around me.

In elementary school, I had friends that I'd grown up with. I was smart and friendly. I was even voted fifth grade class president. But when I transitioned to middle school, around the time I started reading these books and slipped into perversion, I remember feeling like I needed to adjust myself in order to fit people's expectations of me. This would inevitably lead to low self-worth, because I spent more time online in fantasy worlds than I did learning how to actually interact with the new people in my real world. I had a very skewed perspective of how I was "supposed" to be, so I was trying to live up to this idealized version of myself that never really existed. Most middle school kids just want to fit in, but I didn't just want to fit in. It wasn't enough for me to go unnoticed; I *needed* to be liked as much as others. Because I was so unsure of who I was, I began to depend on other people to affirm me. I needed validation from my peers, parents, or teachers at all times to make sure I was living up to this unreasonably high standard. But oftentimes, the validation wasn't enough for me to genuinely feel worthy.

The dangerous part about not knowing who you are and why you're valuable is that it causes you to take on identities that do not belong to you. That low sense of self-worth made me very sensitive to what people said about me or how they spoke to me. When that hypersensitivity was met with unfiltered critique, I was destined to take it personally. I was unable to differentiate between correction and characterization. When I was reprimanded by my parents for losing things or being forgetful, I accepted that I was a careless and irresponsible person. I took it on as an identity. When friends made fun of me for taking a bit longer to process things or for seeing the world in a different way, "slow" and "silly" became parts of my identity. I knew the people around me didn't mean to define me by what was wrong with me, but that hypersensitive girl took it personally.

I don't want to play the victim here. Most of the time, nothing that was said was abusive or even untrue. But the combination of a lack of compassion in their words and my own personal struggles with insecurity led me to feel like *I* was what was wrong with me, especially because I couldn't figure out how to be better. I didn't know how to fix myself. No matter how hard I tried, I kept making the same mistakes and receiving the same criticism. Instead of taking the critique as something I could improve on, I took it on as part of my identity.

Repeating this pattern over the years brought me to a place where I was prone to take everything as a personal indictment of who I was. I went a step further to infer unspoken disapproval based on a lack of attention. I had given people the power to define me for so long that I had come to rely on positive affirmations in order to feel good about myself. But negative comments—or even none at all—made me feel unworthy.

My core issue was one of misplaced identity. At an age when I was just beginning to understand who I was, what other people thought of me felt much more valid than what I thought of myself. Because I hadn't learned to love myself, I internalized both the good and bad that was projected onto me by other people. Everyone does this to some extent. We take cues about ourselves from the communities around us; it's a part of growing up. But whenever we begin to value the opinions of others as superior to God's and use them definitively, it leads to false identities that prevent us from being the people God created us to be. If we live for the approval of others, then we'll die from their rejection.

In some ways, I was dying inside because the books I had read convinced me that my ability to gain approval from others was connected to my value as a person. I spent so much time trying to be the girl I thought I should be that I had absolutely no idea how to be myself. I remember wanting a certain brand of shirts in middle school because they were popular, but I never stopped to think about whether I actually liked them or not. If I thought a friend or a boy really liked me, then I felt valuable. I felt fine about my full name—Oluwasijibomi—until the other kids started to tease me relentlessly about it. I didn't think there was anything wrong with my friends until I heard someone else call us lame. I remember doing silly things like putting tissue paper in my bra because I wasn't developing as fast as the other girls and I wanted attention from boys, too.

Looking back at it, I realize that every emotion I had and every action I took was completely in response to someone else. It didn't even have to be how they actually perceived me, it just had to be how I thought they were responding to me. The reality didn't matter; all that mattered was my perception of reality. But my perception was skewed by a deep sense of shame and insecurity, so I was completely at the mercy of my emotions. Every action I took was specifically planned based on how I thought others would receive it. From what I wore to who I hung out with, from my extracurricular activities to my behavior in school, everything I did was tailored to please others.

One could say I was just being a normal kid. While that might be true, normal behavior isn't always right behavior. If we don't address toxic behaviors that seem normal as children, then we'll become adults with "normal" problematic behaviors that we accept as part of our identities instead of rightly seeing them as flaws we can surrender to God. Just because a problem is common doesn't make it any less of a problem.

Recently, God opened my eyes to show me that I didn't used to be so lost in what other people thought of me. In fact, I didn't pick up that trait until I started reading sexually explicit content and keeping secrets. Because I was suppressing something I was so deeply ashamed of, I was afraid to discover what I might find if I truly got to know myself. So rather than honestly trying to understand my identity, I found it easier to conform to whatever version of myself the people around me liked the most. I didn't trust myself. I filtered all my decisions through the lens of what someone else thought, and I was always inclined to give more credit to the critical opinion of myself. I always felt like I needed to change or adapt in some way. Even so, I never told anyone what I was unsure or insecure about because it didn't fit into the narrative I had created for myself.

This pattern persisted into my early years of high school. All throughout my adolescence, I suffered from acne. I had started breaking out at eleven years old, and it only got worse over time. There were times I would stay at home or be more withdrawn because of it, and no one could convince me that my acne wasn't the first thing people saw when they looked at me. A few people made negative comments or bullied me about my skin, and those were the things that I took to heart and used to understand how every other person must be seeing me.

I suppressed a lot of negative emotions because I wanted to come across as confident, self-assured, and likable. The way I wanted to be perceived took precedence over how I actually felt. I ended up constantly wearing a mask, presenting one version of myself to the world while hiding the real me so thoroughly that even I couldn't recognize her at times. Eventually, it got too hard to differentiate who I was from who I was pretending to be, and the pretense became my personality. It got so bad that even when I was alone I was thinking about what others might think of my actions, despite the fact that they would never know. All of this happened subconsciously until I looked up one day and realized I had no idea who I was.

At one point during sophomore year of high school, I stopped and thought to myself, *Who are you? Who is actually underneath this person who has been nothing more than a walking mirror, simply reflecting everyone's likes and dislikes? If I shattered the mirror and it broke into a million pieces, what would be left? If I wasn't made up of the opinions of others, would I cease to exist?* I remember being so miserably aware that I was controlled by what other people thought. It was paralyzing because I knew what was wrong, but I didn't know how to be free from it. I knew what I was supposed to believe, but I couldn't figure out how to get my mind on board.

Because I had gotten my identity from creations instead of the Creator, I had no idea what I was supposed to do. More importantly, I had no idea who I was supposed to be. I wanted to see myself, know myself, and love myself without factoring the perceptions of others into my decisions, but I had no idea where to start.

Three

THE PRODIGAL DAUGHTER

Death can't have her not yet
Not like this,
Not right now
The change cuts through her
Draining out the old life
From her faintly beating heart
The darkness is absolute now—a tangible thing
She surrenders to the transformation
She sees only darkness

G rowing up, I always wondered what it was like to be on fire for God. I always heard about people who were sold out for Jesus. I wondered what it must be like for those whose lives were radically

transformed by salvation. For me and most of the people I knew, saying the prayer of salvation was simply a rite of passage. We were all born and raised in the church. We loved Jesus, but we loved him in the way you love a grandparent you've never met. We heard about him all our lives. We grew up with stories of him and the idea of him was always there—comfortable and comforting. But, he was given to us before we even knew how to accept him, so when we got to the age of accountability, it seemed as though the only option was Christ. We knew of Jesus in the abstract, so we were able to create customized saviors, gods of our own choosing, who allowed us to call ourselves Christian while having hearts and desires that weren't at all submitted to Christ. We understood sin simply as rule-breaking, so we felt oppressed by the burden of being young Christians, saddled by a religion that seemed only to deprive us of freedom and fun. We desired the security of salvation and the blessings of Christianity, but we craved the excitement and expression of the world. We had this duality down to a science. We knew how to act Christian, and our performances were extremely convincing—after all, we had excellent examples to base them on. Although the church had our devotion, the world had our attention.

I remember being a teenager and thinking about how I couldn't wait to get out of my parents' house and do what

I wanted. I thought that if I was no longer shackled to the rules of their strict, Nigerian, Christian household, then I could have the space to stretch out and discover who I really was. I figured Christianity was good and safe, but it was also so boring and predictable. I couldn't fathom how the other young Christians at church camp were so willing to sacrifice their whole lives to follow this strict set of rules before they actually had the chance to discover what they loved and who they were. I distinctly remember thinking that I wanted the chance to find my identity before I started to take Christianity really seriously. But I had no idea that outside of Christ, I'd only find shallow shells of who I was created to be. It wasn't my parents' fault; they were simply trying to protect me from evils I didn't understand and train me up in the way of the Lord. All the right seeds were planted, but a few too many lies had the chance to root themselves down in my heart beforehand. Religion wasn't enough; I needed a relationship. To put it even more plainly—Christianity wasn't enough; I needed Christ.

When I was in high school, I thought that God and His rules would always be there, but while I was still young and fly, I should be able to experience everything the world had to offer. I didn't want to abandon my faith. I truly believed in Jesus and I was saved; I just figured there had to be a way to balance these two parts of myself—the part that wanted to please my family and church community and the part that wanted to be accepted by friends and the culture. Like many young Christians, I wanted both. I wasn't trying to be a hypocrite; I was simply trying to be happy. I knew I wasn't happy in church, so instead of understanding that I'd just been seeing God wrong, I concluded that God was wrong. At least that's how I acted. I cherry-picked which parts of the faith were easy to obey because I figured that God could wait until I was older to expect complete devotion. I wanted it all, and the pleasures of society seemed to be just out of reach if I took my faith too seriously.

Older Christians in my life told me that the world had nothing good to give me, but it felt ridiculous to take their word for it. I had such a flawed understanding of grace and perfect love that I figured God would be there when I was done exploring and ready to be serious with my faith. I didn't understand that, outside of His presence, I was just creating more scars for God to heal later. I didn't necessarily want to be promiscuous or rebellious; I just figured that there had to be more to life than this tiny box that Christianity would allow me to discover. My curiosity wasn't a bad thing; it was simply misunderstood—even by me. I thought the world must have so much more to offer than a boring Christian life. I never imagined that Jesus

could actually offer me the world. I had no understanding that the longing I felt to discover myself could be satisfied in a God-given identity. I didn't know the loneliness that plagued me could only be lifted in the divine community of my Creator. I didn't understand that while I was searching for belonging and happiness and purpose, I'd never actually find it unless I stopped looking around and looked up.

. . .

In some ways, I think I was in an even more precarious position than a person who is obviously, visibly very far from God. My lack of faith was especially dangerous because everything looked fine from the outside. I had mastered the art of being whatever version of myself I thought would get the most approval. I was my church's youth president. I was a good kid, a straight-A student, and I never got into any real trouble. I volunteered on weekends and tried to be respectful to adults. I was frustrated by the rules, but I followed them anyway—knee-length skirts, home by 10:00 p.m., and quiet and respectful. But none of those things made me a Christian, because

Christ didn't have my heart yet. Those actions were what I wanted my parents and youth teachers to see. However, when my friends made fun of me for being so straight-edge, I talked down about the very things I seemed so committed to moments before. I made it seem like the whole good-girl act was just for show to survive my parents' household so I could really start living when I got to college.

Meanwhile, I still desired the kind of romance I read about. I'd been conditioned to believe the lie that my beauty and desirability were directly related to how many guys liked me or complimented me. I distinctly remember feeling like I wasn't beautiful, because surely if I was, someone would have mentioned it to me. I picked myself apart, analyzing everything that was wrong with me—from my blemished skin, to my childish body, to my crooked smile. I unknowingly convinced myself that because I wasn't the prettiest, I wasn't pretty at all. Because I didn't get attention from guys, I was somehow unattractive.

It was such a twisted way to think, but it wasn't something I consciously chose to believe. It was just something that I subconsciously accepted because of what I'd been exposed to. My life was a puzzle, and each piece was a contradiction. I wanted so desperately to be loved, to feel seen and understood. But I was so busy trying to be

everything for everyone else that I became nothing to myself. I knew something was missing, but from the outside looking in it appeared like everything was fine, so I went along with that narrative.

The truth is, I was the prodigal son. However, I had not yet become the more infamous younger son who runs away, reckless and rebellious with his inheritance. I was not yet the son who stands as a lavish representation of God's unmerited grace. I was the *other* prodigal son—the one who gets far less attention in the retelling of this parable.

I was the older son who stayed home and did everything right but still had a heart that was far from the Father (Luke 15:11-32). My relationship with God was transactional. I figured that if I did all the right things, then He would owe me a good life. I would allow Jesus to be the Savior of my spirit, but he could never be the Lord of my mind, heart, and soul, because that position was already filled by me. I had a great outward posture but a terrible heart posture because I knew that the grace of God was free, but I didn't understand why I needed it. I thought I was so good that I couldn't recognize how far away I was. How on earth does a sick person seek healing if they believe the symptoms of their sickness are perfectly normal? It is only those who know they are dying who can choose life. This is why the

Bible says the Gospel "…is foolishness to those who are perishing" (1 Corinthians 1:18 NIV).

During junior year of high school, my distinct lack of relationship with God began to make itself more apparent. Although I didn't know it at the time, the declining state of my mental health was an indicator that something was wrong. I logically knew my life was fine. I was blessed with nothing other than first-world problems and adolescent drama. But there was a deep restlessness inside of me. No matter how hard I tried to put my life into perspective, joy evaded me and my happiness was fleeting. I started to experience periods of overwhelming, inexplicable sadness. I figured no one would understand the crushing loneliness I felt or the depression that overwhelmed me for months at a time, because I didn't understand it myself. I couldn't articulate how agonizing it felt to be crippled by the weight of what people might think of me. My life looked great on paper, but I switched so frequently between feeling broken and feeling fine that the dysfunction in my mind became my new normal.

I knew something was wrong, but I never connected it to my spiritual life. I eventually realized there was a gaping hole where purpose and identity were supposed to be, but that seemed like something I needed to sort through by myself. I was technically doing all the right Christian things,

so I could never have imagined that my problem was a God-shaped chasm in my life. I really thought Jesus and I were cool. I believed in him. I served him. I prayed to him. I even fasted once in a while with my church. However, I didn't understand how to go to him with my pain and shame. Even though I was always around the things of God, my heart was far from Him. The God I knew was the God of rules, regulations, and religion. It wasn't all bad, though. He was also the God of my family, my community, and my success. But He wasn't God of *my* pain or *my* joy or *my* identity. I was broken, and God only got a few fractured pieces of me at a time. Therefore, I continuously cut myself on the jagged edges of my wicked heart because I didn't know how to accept the impenetrable love of a good God.

I saw reflections of God in the faith of my parents, but I couldn't see God for myself. I knew about God from a lifetime of growing up in the church, but I didn't know the God of the Bible on a personal level. I loved the idea of God in theory, but my understanding of love was so shallow that I had no idea how to love Him in practice. When you've only met the people of God and you've never encountered the person of God, you find yourself living trapped in religion instead of free in salvation. Without an encounter with the person behind the religion, your liberation will always look like captivity and your blessings will always appear to be bondage. Because I believed in a Savior who I'd never gotten to know intimately, I had no reference point for what it really meant to be free in Christ. Christianity was something I did, not who I was. My soul was saved but my life wasn't transformed.

...

I knew I had a problem, but years went by until I had any idea how to address it, because I didn't have a revelation of what was at the root. Can you imagine? Years of not knowing my purpose, existing simply to please everyone around me, craving attention as an indicator that I mattered to someone in some way. I'm not saying I was completely miserable the whole time. For the most part, I was a normal, high-achieving, young Nigerian girl on the outside. I had loving parents and a supportive community. But what people didn't see was the girl on the inside who felt a deep, overwhelming loneliness and fear of rejection. They didn't see the girl who went through cycles of depression. They didn't see the girl who used to sob into her pillow at night, crying to God that she just wanted to be happy.

It was a long time before I was far enough from those experiences of sexual perversion as a child to look back and see what they had done to the fundamental ways I saw myself and the world. I was several experiences and many truths away from understanding the impact it had on my life. There's a way in which your innocence sometimes prevents you from understanding the genesis of your problem. The inappropriate books I had read on that website when I was younger never even crossed my mind when I first realized I had low self-esteem or when I recognized I had an unhealthy desire for the attention of men. It was through the process of writing this book and meditating on scriptures, like Psalm 139, that God began to show me the lies that stood behind my thoughts and the feelings which led to toxic, sinful patterns. There's a reason why the devil is known as the father of lies. It was all connected, and I had no idea.

The problem I had is the same one that a lot of us have. It's not that I wasn't taught about faith and how I should see myself and others. It was that all my lessons were stacked on top of a fundamental misunderstanding of God. The seeds of my world view were rooted in the soil of perversion. So when the sunlight and rain of good upbringing and Godly instruction caused the tree of my life to grow, the fruit I produced was a little off. It tasted funny.

The growth of the fruit was stunted because, even though no one above ground could see it, I was growing from rotten roots. There were things I believed to be true about myself at such a fundamental level that I assumed they were just a part of who I was meant to be. I genuinely thought I wasn't enough. Yes, we are born in sin and shaped in iniquity, but I couldn't understand why I still struggling so much to change my thoughts after I'd supposedly been reborn, transformed, and made new in Christ.

...

During late high school, no matter how many times I told myself I was fearfully and wonderfully made, no matter how many friends told me I was gorgeous, I couldn't really believe it. No matter how many times my parents emphasized my worth, I found it impossible to truly accept it myself. Maybe for a few days, when my skin was clear of acne or in times when I was distracted. But not consistently, not for real.

As a teenager, I grew so frustrated with myself because I knew that I was looking for a man—or better yet, men—to affirm my worth so I could prove I had value. *If I'm really*

beautiful, then why don't men feel compelled to tell me the way they tell my friends? I would think. I thought I had a beautiful soul and a beautiful mind, but I didn't just want to appear beautiful after a long conversation. I wanted to be seen as make-a-man-stop-in-his-tracks-and-double-back attractive. I wanted to have a beauty that made hearts ache. I wanted men to say, "Yeah, I'll stop and get to know her personality later, but my goodness, look at her face!"

Even still, I knew better. I had been taught that those things didn't really matter in the end. I understood intellectually that my desires were misplaced but that didn't make them any less real. I was stuck in a place where I didn't like myself because even though I knew better, I couldn't figure out how to be better. Due to that original perversion of love and lust at age eleven, my desires were terribly controlled by the male gaze, and it led to years of deep insecurity. I know what you're thinking. Trust me, I told myself constantly that I should just love myself more. People always say that, but they never tell you how. If it was as easy as just making the decision, then I'm sure we wouldn't need to be reminded so often. I had no clue how to be who I thought I was supposed to be. Since I started from a place of deception, I could not get my heart to believe what my mind already knew to be true.

I was raised in two schools of thought. One taught me that I was worth the world, worthy of intrinsic value no matter what any man has to say about it. The other taught me a contradictory story that grew stronger because of those rotten roots. It told me that my acne-ridden face, my crooked smile, my too-far-apart eyes, and my untamable hair were simply unappealing. It taught me that my beauty was categorized and defined by men. Even though I knew this was wrong in my mind, my heart wasn't able to recover from what I had been conditioned to believe. Therefore, like anything that doesn't want to be held up to the sky for fear that the sun will illuminate all the flaws that make it unpretty, I hid in darkness. I hid out of fear that if the whole of me was cast into stark relief against the backdrop of something more stunning, I would be ridiculed for my sad attempts to be seen.

I thought I wanted to be seen, but what I really wanted was to be known. It is a desire we all have, and it comes from God. It gives us the capacity to enter into intimacy with Him and others. However, in this fallen world, that good desire has been flipped and directed downwards. We look to other people for that which we can only really receive in the presence of God. So now, we find ourselves here attempting, like mother Eve and father Adam, to hide in plain sight under the broad daylight of God's glory. We are dimmed timelines presenting partial selves to the world while rejecting the Creator who is the only one capable of loving every single broken part of us.

Many of the ways we reject God and hide from Him are subconscious, hidden under the ground of our seemingly innocent decisions, like roots of lies buried long ago—out of sight, but constantly corrupting the mind. The danger comes when we think we have good perceptions of ourselves, so we are unprepared when a lack of attention, toxic social media comparison, hurtful words from family, and rejection by friends and lovers reveal the many cracks in our identities.

We pridefully try to patch up our damaged identities by presenting filtered versions of ourselves or striving to please other imperfect people. Are you less gorgeous because you're the only one who's noticed your beauty? Are you less of a man because the blanket of security laid out in the form of your career and image hasn't gotten you the respect you expected? If you turn other people's opinions of you into mirrors that reflect back your own value, you'll always see a lie.

Sometimes, we believe that we think highly of ourselves, but then we find ourselves repeating the same faulty scripts of "I'm so weird," and "I'm so dumb," and "I am so big."

Why is it that we find it so hard to really believe the truth we know about ourselves?

I knew I had value and worth. I knew I was uniquely and beautifully designed. I'd known this for some time, but how was I supposed to transfer that knowledge to a place of belief? The knowledge that my self-esteem was low and should be high didn't move that self-esteem any higher. Loved ones told me to pray, and I did, but I still had all the symptoms of my sickness because I hadn't discovered the cure. The only improvement in my condition came when I finally realized I was ill.

First, God revealed to me that there were still some things I needed to unlearn. One of the most insidious things the devil did was take advantage of my God-given curiosity as a child so that I settled for the first answers I stumbled upon rather than answers that were rooted in Truth. Many people like to believe that truth is subjective and varies based on experience, but when we critically examine this idea, we find that it is false. If your idea of truth directly contradicts mine, then how can we both be right? Without God, there is no basis for anchoring your life on anything concrete, because if one person's truth is just as valid as anyone else's, then right and wrong cease to mean anything. One of the most important things about constantly learning is that we are constantly able to refine

our ideas; however, if our entire frame of reference is wrong, then we're simply getting closer and closer to the wrong answer.

Godly thoughts about myself didn't have anywhere to take root because the soil of my mind was overrun by the weeds of a false reality. I was like the person, who Jesus describes in the parable of the sower, whose heart was filled with thorny soil which deceitfully choked out the seeds of the Gospel and made the Christian life unfruitful (Matthew 13:22). Although I had cut down the trees of perversion and deception, the seeds of transformation couldn't grow to produce a changed life because I had never dealt with the rotten roots. God doesn't just want to heal our symptoms; He wants to eradicate the disease. Ezekiel 36:26 (NLT) says, "And I will give you a new heart, and I will put a new spirit in you. I will take out your stony, stubborn heart and give you a tender, responsive heart." His mission is not just to repair; it is to replace. However, I could never truly be free until I chose to surrender. I had allowed myself to be miseducated by lustful thoughts and ungodly desires. I had been curious about who I would be if I wasn't limited by the rules of religion, but I needed to get curious about who I might become if I was set free through a relationship with Jesus. I had to begin unlearning the lies if I was ever going to believe the truth.

The Prodigal Daughter

- Four -

THE ROOTS

And then gradually,
Yet all at once,
Rebirth
I see, I feel,
The life, The light
I squint at the glare of a new day
The irresistible glow takes ahold of my soul
The pain here is a stunning reminder that I am alive

dmitting the extent of my insecurity was a good first step, but in order to be free, I had to dig even deeper. The truth is there were three things behind my insecurity:

1. I had a **pride** problem.
2. I had an *identity* problem.
3. I had a **fear of man** problem.

PRIDE

I was so deeply insecure because I was so prideful. It wasn't the pride of thinking I was better than everyone else. It was the pride of believing I was less than I deserved to be. I know this thinking may sound a little contradictory, but Edward T. Welch explains it well in his book, *When People Are Big and God is Small*, when he states:

> Low self-esteem usually means that I think too highly of myself. I am too self-involved, I feel I deserve better than what I have. The reason I feel bad about myself is that I aspire to something more. I just want a few minutes of greatness. I am a peasant who wants to be a king. When you are in the grips of low self-esteem, it's painful and it certainly doesn't feel like pride. But I

believe that this is the dark, quieter side of pride—thwarted pride.[2]

I didn't realize it consciously until God opened my eyes, but underneath my low self-esteem was the idea that I *deserved* to fit in and be accepted by the people I admired. I thought I *deserved* to have a personality that brought lots of close, intimate friendships. I *deserved* to have beautiful, clear skin and straight teeth. I *deserved* better than I had. I thought the world owed me something. But since I was not the way I wanted to be—nor the way I thought I deserved to be—I was unhappy. I didn't consciously think about it like that, but that was the underlying reason. Low self-esteem motivated by pride is not only disliking what you have, but also feeling entitled to more. That's why it goes hand in hand with comparison.

I was constantly trying to find fault in others because I was miserably aware of my own faults and felt entitled to the beauty, relationships, and success I saw in others. Most of the time, our ideas of what we deserve are developed in comparison to others. We don't realize that even though God made us perfectly equal, He also made us perfectly unique. Psalm 139:14 (NIV) says that we are "fearfully and

---

[2] Welch, Edward T. *When People Are Big and God Is Small.* P & R Publishing, 1997.

wonderfully made," but the Bible also says, "No one is righteous—not even one. No one is truly wise; no one is seeking God. All have turned away; all have become useless (Romans 3:10-12 NLT).

The reality check I had to experience is that although I am fearfully and wonderfully made, I am still just a sinner saved by grace. Anything that God has chosen to bless me with is simply a reflection of His undeserved favor and mercy. It points to His goodness, not mine. For me to then demand more than that favor and mercy—like I've done anything at all to deserve it—is just like telling God that He isn't as knowing or as good as He claims to be. It's calling God's character into question by asserting that I know more than Him. If I'm not mistaken, that was the exact sin of Satan.

I was prideful to think that the specific way I was created by God wasn't enough for me. I saw myself as less, but not less than what God made me. I saw myself as less than what I had gassed myself up to be because I didn't think the way God made me was good enough. Therefore, you could say that in my insecurity, I was looking down on myself. However, that meant I had exalted myself to a higher level than I really was in the first place. After all, you can only look down on something if you're above it.

That exalted level is the place of pride. God is the only one who can look down and see things clearly. Humans need to face reality head-on, because when we look at ourselves and others from a place of pride, we have a warped view of what we think is below us.

The Bible says in Psalm 8:5 (NLT) that we were made just "a little lower than God." However, because we are all made equally in His image, no one person is higher than anyone else. Our character can improve, but our inherent value will never change. When we keep our eyes fixed on God and really see Him for who He is, then we have the proper reference point for every human being, including ourselves.

You see, without God, we are really just walking, talking sacks of clay. Unless His life force animates us, we're basically empty. The only thing that has enough substance to fill us up is God. But pride tricks us into thinking we can be filled by all sorts of earthly things. Pride tells us we can single-handedly fill or satisfy ourselves. The problem is, you are not enough for yourself—not even close. If you are full of yourself, you might as well be empty.

James 4:6 (NLT) says, "God opposes the proud but gives grace to the humble." God opposes proud people for several reasons, but I would have to imagine one of those reasons is because they look incredibly foolish. They go around displaying how they are filled up with wealth, accomplishments, or friends when they are very obviously empty.

In Ephesians 3:18-19 (TPT), Paul's prayer to the church in Ephesus is:

> ...Then you will be empowered to discover what every holy one experiences—the great magnitude of the astonishing love of Christ in all its dimensions. How deeply intimate and far-reaching is his love! How enduring and inclusive it is! Endless love beyond measurement that transcends our understanding—this extravagant love pours into you until you are filled to overflowing with the fullness of God!

So you see, to really live free from pride is to have a life so filled with the love and presence of God that it makes us whole. Imagine the fullness of the all-knowing, perfectly good Creator of the universe. Imagine the awe-inspiring magnitude of His love. There is the hope of being filled up with that, if only we would choose it. Yet, we desperately try to find transient, worthless, inadequate things to fill us up so we can feel good about ourselves. God is saying, "Stop worrying about *feeling* good about who you are; focus on *being* good because of the goodness of God in you." You should feel good about yourself—that desire isn't wrong—but God is the only one who can give permanent self-worth because He is the ultimate foundation of our worth.

The Holy Spirit taught me that my love for who I am had to come from the understanding of *whose* I am. I was so focused on myself—if I was good enough, smart enough, pretty enough, and engaging enough. I wondered, *What is wrong with me? What do other people think about me?* I wondered about how other people looked at me—me, me, me! How could I possibly see God when I was so obsessed with looking at myself? I could tell myself that I was special, beautiful, and worthy all day, but it wouldn't work because that wasn't the problem. The problem was pride. I was entirely too consumed with myself to believe the truth about myself. The disease was pride, and the treatment was a heavy dose of humility.

In *The Purpose Driven Life*, Rick Warren writes, "Humility is not thinking less of yourself, it's thinking of yourself less."[3] When I first read this, it blew my mind. It stopped me dead in my tracks because I'd been viciously fighting the symptoms of my insecurity for years, but I wasn't getting better because I never dealt with the disease of

---

[3] Warren, Rick. *The Purpose Driven Life.* Zondervan, 2002.

pride. However, like so many people, I misunderstood what humility means.

So many of us think humility means having a low view of yourself. But that doesn't seem to make sense for someone who is trying to increase their self-esteem. I would argue that humility is really having the *proper* view of yourself. Not any lower than it should be and not any higher than it needs to be. Just accurate. In the same way that you can never understand a book if you only focus on a single sentence, you can never understand your worth by just focusing on yourself. It seems counterintuitive until you realize you aren't the full story. You might be a supporting character, but who is more important: the character in a novel, or the author of the novel? If you're not sure what the right answer is, think about how many times you've seen a Nobel Prize given to the character in a book. No matter how brilliantly that character speaks and thinks and acts, it can't be more impressive than the author who created it. The character may be beloved, but at the end of the day when the book closes, the author gets all the glory and praise for his or her creation. God is *The* Author, and in order to properly appreciate our value as characters, we must look to the person who created our narrative. He's the perfect writer, the only writer, and He cannot make mistakes.

When I take my eyes off of myself long enough to see God, not just as righteous and holy, but as beautiful, I come to a place of humility. In this place, I can see myself for exactly who I am—a daughter of God, made in His image, and created to give Him glory.

IDENTITY

/ ˌīˈden(t)ədē/
Noun

1. the fact of being who or what a person or thing is.[4]
2. the distinguishing character or personality of an individual[5]
3. who a person is, or the qualities of a person or group that makes them different from others[6]

---

[4] Identity (n.d.). *The language data is provided by Oxford Languages, part of Oxford University Press.*
[5] Identity. In *Merriam-Webster.com*. Retrieved May 21, 2021, from www.merriam-webster.com/dictionary/identity
[6] Identity. In *Cambridge Dictionary*. Retrieved May 21, 2021, from dictionary.cambridge.org/us/dictionary/english/identity

We all have identities in Christ that are different from the identities the world often tries to give us. While I was looking for approval and attention by constantly adapting to everyone around me, God was there loving the real me, not who I was pretending to be. There is a saying that goes, "God can't bless who you pretend to be." This is true, but it's even more convincing when you realize that while you're pretending to be who you think you're supposed to be, God is literally blessing the person He made you to be. When you step into who you were created to be, you step into the blessings and grace that God already ordained for you before the foundations of the earth.

While I was trying to be who I thought I was supposed to be, God was waiting for me to realize that He is the only one who has the power to define me, and the name He's given me is Image-Bearer: Imago Dei.

So God created mankind in his own image,
in the image of God he created them;
male and female he created them.

(Genesis 1:27 NIV)

The Bible tells me that I am a beloved daughter made in the image of my Father. God is therefore the only one who can love and accept me the way that I need. He is the only one who can love me like that before I even try to earn it. He loves me perfectly, but God is so good that He is also working to sanctify me so I can become more like Christ. He isn't just waiting; He is divinely orchestrating my realization of His faithfulness. He gave Himself up so He could show me, practically, what love looks like.

Because I didn't know my identity, I was missing out on being the person who could receive that love. It was as if I was running away from myself. When I finally came back to myself, it was by coming back to God. I was so lost that I didn't realize I was lost, much less how to get back home. All that time I was out there, existing in fragments rather than living whole. So, broken and filled with holes, I went to God and He put me back together again. Since He made me, He was the only one who knew how I was supposed to be. He restored me to factory settings. I thought I loved God, but because I hadn't allowed His love for me to define who I was, I was physically incapable of loving Him well or allowing His love to really change me. The whole time I was trying to be someone else, He was right there loving the real me.

Identity is a very biblical concept. The aim of the Bible is to lead us to Jesus. Throughout the Gospels, specifically in John, the Bible makes a point of ensuring that we are able to identify Jesus as the Son of God. This has to be the beginning of our understanding of who God is, who we are, and who others are. Understanding your identity begins with understanding the identity of Christ.

Jesus spent most of his life knowing who he was while few others recognized him. He didn't become the Messiah because others identified him as the Messiah; he was always the Messiah because that is who God created him to be. When John baptized him, John received the revelation that Jesus was the son of God. John and Jesus were family members, but John did not recognize Jesus' identity until they were both grown. If Jesus had waited for others to affirm his identity, he would never have been prepared to let the world know exactly who he was when the time came.

We must not define our identities based on what other people say about us. How can people who only see the outside know us better than the God who made the inside? The God who made you and gave you purpose is the only one who has the ability to define you. Who you are is not who people say you are. Oftentimes, you are not even who you think you are; you are who God made you to be. Until you align your identity for yourself with God's identity for you, you will never truly know your God-given purpose.

In my journey towards healing, I realized that my prayer must change from, "God, make me the best version of myself," to, "God, let me live as who you've created me to be." As the saying goes, "All I have is all I need." There isn't some distant, ultimate self at the end of your journey in life. Your existence is not a game with levels through which you claim the best version of yourself as a prize. You don't have to search for it. Outside things can develop you, but your best potential already exists within you. God is the key to unlocking it.

We are all fallen at birth, but throughout life, so many layers of lies and confusion get piled on top of us. We're constantly taking on ideas, behaviors, and habits so antithetical to who God called us to be that we get to the point where we're unrecognizable as who God created. But that person is still there; they are just covered up. The reason it felt like I was so unqualified when God called me is that He's already equipped me with everything that will qualify me. I was born with it; I simply had no idea that it was there. In *Gay Girl, Good God,* Jackie Hill Perry writes:

It is the identity that we ascribe to God out of doubt or faith in his Scriptures that will determine the identity we will give ourselves and ultimately the life that we inevitably live. If he is the Creator, then we are created. If he is Master, then we are servants. If he is love, then we are loved. If he is omnipotent, then we are not as powerful as we think. If he is omniscient, then there is nowhere to hide. If he cannot lie, then his promises are all true. It is faith in the truths of God's character that has the power to completely revolutionize how our lives are lived out.[7]

It was hard to see, much less claim, my identity when it was so hidden by the persona I took on in an attempt to be worthy in the eyes of the world. It was never hidden to God, though. God knew me better than I knew myself, and He knows you too. He still sees everything that He placed in you when He created you. When God looks at you, He sees who He made. He sees who you are, not the cocoon of deception that the world built around you. Once you realize this, you'll be able to measure everything you think you know about yourself against the Truth that you know in God. You'll be able to identify as the Imago Dei, the image of God, the person He created you to be.

---

[7] Perry, Jackie Hill. *Gay Girl, Good God*. B&H Books, 2018.

FEAR OF MAN

Connected to both my pride and misplaced identity was a deep sense of fear. At my core, I was afraid of what people would think of me if they really knew me. I cared so much about what people thought because I was afraid of being exposed. Deep down, I was still that embarrassed and ashamed little girl doing things under her covers at night, things that she was convinced made her a bad person. My shame was birthed from the depths of my sin and made me fear other people in a way that I should have only feared God. I needed people to like me or approve of me because I was afraid that if they didn't, then what I'd suspected all along would be true. I was afraid that if I didn't receive love from others, then it would confirm the fact that I wasn't worthy of love. It would prove that I deserved to be alone.

But, according to Brené Brown's definition, shame is powered by the belief that what we do or don't do determines whether we're worthy of connection. She says that shame is, "The intensely painful feeling or experience of believing that we are flawed and therefore unworthy of love and belonging—something we've experienced, done, or failed to do makes us unworthy of connection."[8]

---

[8] Brown, Brené. *The Gifts of Imperfection*. Simon and Schuster, 2010.

According to this definition of shame, if something can make us unworthy of connection, then something else can make us worthy of connection. This can only be true if our worth is based on something fickle like the fleeting acceptance of others instead of the immaculate image of God.

Edward T. Welch says:

Fear in the biblical sense is a much broader word. It includes being afraid of someone, but it extends to holding someone in awe, being controlled or mastered by other people, worshipping other people, putting your trust in people, or needing people… **Fear of man can be summarized in this way: We replace God with other people, instead of biblically guided fear of the Lord, we fear others.**[9]

When I experienced shame, it was because I felt that other people could make me worthy or unworthy. I only believed that because I unintentionally gave them the power to determine something that God has already decided—my value. If I am afraid of failing, then I am controlled by success. If I am afraid of being unloved, then

---

[9] Welch, Edward T. *When People Are Big and God Is Small.* P & R Publishing, 1997.

I am controlled by the love of others. If I am afraid of disapproval, then I am controlled by approval. Whatever we put our worth in is what we truly fear. Fear of man means I have given people or circumstances the power to determine what I believe about myself.

We often strive desperately for success, love, or approval in hopes of proving our worth and silencing the shame that tells us we are not enough. I've learned that fear is the father of shame. With my fear of man, I allowed others to determine what I thought I was worth, and as fear ruled over me, shame was always lurking in the shadows.

When Adam and Eve sinned in the Garden of Eden, they were ashamed of their behavior. They felt that something they did made them unworthy of connection, so they hid from God. However, the Bible also says they hid their nakedness from each other. Why would they hide from each other if they sinned against God? Before that sin, before the fall of man, they had a pure and undefiled fear of God. Their sin wasn't just the disobedience of eating the fruit; it was the motivation behind that action. Genesis 3:1-7 (NLT) spells it out:

> The serpent was the shrewdest of all the wild animals the Lord God had made. One day he asked the woman, "Did God really say you must not eat the fruit from any

of the trees in the garden?" "Of course we may eat fruit from the trees in the garden," the woman replied. "It's only the fruit from the tree in the middle of the garden that we are not allowed to eat. God said, 'You must not eat it or even touch it; if you do, you will die." "You won't die!" the serpent replied to the woman. "God knows that your eyes will be opened as soon as you eat it, and you will be like God, knowing both good and evil." The woman was convinced. She saw that the tree was beautiful and its fruit looked delicious, and she wanted the wisdom it would give her. So she took some of the fruit and ate it. Then she gave some to her husband, who was with her, and he ate it, too. At that moment their eyes were opened, and they suddenly felt shame at their nakedness. So they sewed fig leaves together to cover themselves.

We see that at that moment, Adam and Eve didn't just desire the fruit for itself. They wanted it for what it could give them. They wanted to be like God. More specifically, they wanted to be able to define good and evil for themselves. Their fear of missing out on this mysterious knowledge was greater than their fear of disobeying the one who created them, so they were controlled by their desires instead of His. By calling God's goodness into question,

Satan convinced them that they could trust themselves more than God. The moment they chose their own wills over God's, they put themselves in a position of authority that was only meant for Him. However, their small, human egos were not enough to shield them. They weren't big enough to be their own gods.

At this first sin, Adam and Eve removed themselves from the covering of the Most High by disrupting the perfectly submitted relationship they had with Him. Therefore, it is no wonder that they wanted to hide. They were vulnerable and exposed. Outside of the Father's presence, all that was left was their own inadequate humanity, and that wasn't enough. They needed more; they were created for more. They believed their actions made them unworthy of connection with God and each other, so they hid in shame.

People have been making that same mistake ever since. It is the mistake I made as a child and for years after. I sinned and put myself into direct opposition with God. I felt the guilt and shame of knowing I had done something wrong. Even though I didn't have a close relationship with God, He created me with an innate sense of right and wrong. Like most people, instead of running back into the covering of a good God, I ran away. I shrank back from a place that I thought would only bring condemnation.

However, we were designed to fear, be controlled by, trust, and need God and God alone. He created humans to worship, to be reverent, and to submit. When I turned away from God, intentionally or unintentionally, that need to fear something, to worship something, and to submit to something never went away.

As humans, we think we are in control of ourselves, but the truth is there is always something else controlling us. If it is not God, it will be money or power or sex or approval. Because my shame led me out of God's presence, I began to be controlled by inadequate things. I became a perfectionist and people-pleaser, living to fill my emptiness with the praises of others. I not only wanted to be liked, I also needed others' approval because I had put other people in a place of authority and control over my life which was only meant for God. However, mere humans would never be enough for me to worship—they weren't even enough for themselves.

The more I looked to people and accomplishments to make me feel worthy, the more the realities of life made me realize that I made the wrong choice. Just like my ancient ancestors, I tried to hide from the Creator among His creation, but shame creeped in and found me there because I'd placed my fear, my trust, and my desire in the wrong things. While I worshiped at the altar of other people's opinions, I plunged deeper into shame and self-hate.

Growing up, I knew all the while that something was wrong, but when I went to the world for answers, society and culture told me that the solution to my low self-esteem was to have high self-esteem. At the time, it made a lot of sense to me. I didn't love myself enough, so I needed to love myself more. I tried to be confident and self-assured. I tried to affirm myself so I wouldn't need others to affirm me. I focused a lot of mental and emotional energy on the things I was good at, the things I could feel good about, and then displayed them to the world. Since I had nothing solid to base my self-worth on, I began a dangerous cycle of comparison where I felt good about myself when I found someone I was better than. Once again, all of this was subconscious and can be much more clearly seen in hindsight, but it was my reality at the time. I tried to believe that it didn't matter what anyone else thought about me; all that mattered was what I thought about myself.

As you can imagine, this strategy failed horribly. I became an expert at pretending, but deep down inside, I was still the same insecure girl. I put on my disguise every day, terrified that someone would rip off my mask and expose me for who I really was. Instead of solving my problem, I actually made it worse. I not only dealt with the fear of man because of my original sin and shame, I also dealt with the fear of being exposed for all the lies I used to cover up those insecurities.

Remember, insecurity is a side of pride that comes from thinking about yourself too much. By trying to focus so much on developing high self-esteem, I not only thought of myself too much, but in many areas, I really did begin to think of myself as better than other people. Researchers have found that there is both explicit self-esteem—what we say about ourselves—and implicit self-esteem—how we honestly, automatically feel about ourselves. One study found that the combination of high explicit and low implicit self-esteem is sometimes a sign of defensive denial resulting from insecurity. That kind of self-love is, if not inauthentic, at least fragile and unstable, fluctuating as a person anxiously or irritably monitors the reactions of others.[10]

My self-love was for show, but it didn't actually change how I saw myself. I was faking it, but I most definitely was not making it. Both the secular and spiritual world know low self-esteem isn't great; but forcing high self-esteem wasn't the solution, either. So what could I do?

---

[10] Lin Zhang, Quanlei Yu, Qiuying Zhang, Yafei Guo, Jianwen Chen. (2020) The relationship between explicit self-esteem and subjective well-being: The moderating effect of implicit self-esteem. *The Journal of General Psychology* 147:1, pages 1-17.

Trying to fix myself only left me painfully aware of my brokenness, because the whole time I was worried about high self-esteem and low self-esteem, I was being distracted from the real issue. I was making the same mistakes, just in different ways. As a people-pleaser with obviously low self-esteem, I tried to fit in and make people happy so I could win their approval and feel better about myself. As an attention-seeker, I tried to gain high self-esteem by accomplishing a lot socially and academically. But because my standard was other people, I was stuck in a cycle of comparison, constantly trying to prove I was as good and confident as everyone else so I could gain their admiration and feel better about myself. All of my efforts were to *feel* better, but I never once thought about how to *be* better. I needed God-esteem. I needed to see myself the way He sees me: not too high, not too low, but just right—inherently valuable and redeemed in Christ.

Therefore, I couldn't be freed by anything other than the Gospel of Jesus Christ, because while everything else addresses the fruit, God looks at the root. Romans 8:1 (NLT) says, "…there is no condemnation for those who belong to Christ Jesus." Outside of Christ, we are constantly condemned because we *do* sin; we *do* mess up. That feeling of shame reminds us of this. We don't like to hear this, but we've all done things that we should be ashamed of. I've done shameful things because I was born in sin and raised in inequity like everyone else. The problem comes when we take that shame and allow it to define how we see ourselves, others, and most importantly, God. The fear of man made me believe that my shame was bigger than God's grace. Instead of feeling shame as a useful emotion to let me know that I was wrong, I took it on as my identity. Instead of allowing God to tell me who I was, I let my actions tell me who God is.

Like Eve, I had been left exposed and uncovered by shame. I ran away from the fear of God, but the only solution was to go back. If I had to fear someone, why not make it the one worth fearing? Why not fear a God who would never manipulate me or take advantage of me? Why not fear a God who meets my imperfect submission with perfect love?

I must emphasize that this process of learning to fear God is not the same as receiving salvation. Salvation gives you access to His presence. It is the moment of ultimate grace that opens the door to a relationship with God, but continual surrender is what ushers you in and keeps you there. Even when I was in the depths of shame and insecurity, I wasn't a complete neophyte in the faith. I knew a lot about Jesus; I just hadn't surrendered my whole life to him yet. I went into my faith the same way I went into everything else in my life—with the focus on myself. I didn't want Christ for who he was, I wanted him for what he could do for me.

My freedom from the fear of man wasn't going to come from simply being aware of the Gospel; it had to come from living the Gospel. I couldn't just be around God, I had to draw near to Him and abide in Him. John 15:4 (NKJV) says, "Abide in Me, and I in you. As the branch cannot bear fruit of itself, unless it abides in the vine, neither can you, unless you abide in Me."

Even though I was saved, I would continue to bear the bad fruit of shame, fear, and insecurity unless I learned to lean into the presence of God.

The Roots

Five

UPROOTING

I am not strong enough so I rest in my saving grace
The sorrow gives dimension to the joy
The pain makes beauty take shape
The hope stands as light against the backdrop of despair
I was resuscitated as the person I was created to be
The person that had always previously been defined by darkness
I was unable to see her, to know her before
But here she is
finally

ow that we have addressed the roots, I must describe the process I had to go through to become free. It was a journey of pressing into the presence of God, seeking His face, and doing some serious heart work. I had discovered the roots of my insecurity, but the process of uprooting would take divine intervention. As I mentioned before, the issues at the core of my insecurity and warped world view were pride, misplaced identity, and a fear of man that manifested as shame.

During the process of writing this book, when I studied the Word and really pressed in for God to reveal more about the truth of my identity, He took me back to my childhood. He helped me to see that as far back as I could remember, I was outgoing. People would come over to the house, and five-year-old Siji would perform "Survivor" by Destiny's Child in her favorite ruffled cheetah-print shirt and toy sunglasses. I would make up songs and sing at the top of my lungs to my family, basking in their wild applause at my off-tune singing. But mostly, I was just happy to be having fun.

I really thrived in that little bubble of childhood joy until I was about eleven. We've already gone over all the traumatic, terrible seeds that were planted in that season, but one outcome of holding in all that deep shame was that I learned to believe that what was unique about me wasn't so special. I learned that my desire to be in the spotlight and my gift of being able to articulate myself and command attention was not valuable. I couldn't change who I was, so I simply tried to become someone else.

Growing up, the one thing I was good at was school, so I put most of my focus and attention into that. Along with people-pleasing, my academics were where I got my value and self-worth. It seemed too risky to be rebellious in my strict Nigerian household, so I bided my time, excelled academically, and waited until I could leave the house. As my high school graduation grew closer, I felt the anticipation of leaving my home shiver through my bones. There was an intense aching and longing to move away. I placed all my hope, excitement, and desire into that dream of going off to college and finally getting the freedom I needed to find myself.

What I should have realized is that when you go searching for something you have never seen, you're likely to end up with something you never wanted. When I got to the University of Texas at Austin, I realized that I wasn't as smart as I thought and the friends I had hoped to find would not come so easily. I felt lost. I had struggled with depression in high school, but I fell deeper into anxiety and depression in college because the things I used to define myself and cover my shame for so long were abruptly ripped away from me. I was left exposed, afraid, and vulnerable. I had made leaving home a kind of savior to me. It was the one thing I thought would bring me joy after years of sadness, and it let me down completely. In fact, it made things worse because the problem was never my environment, it was me.

During my first few months of college I went through cycles of fighting to be liked and accepted. I would feel satisfied and sanctified for a while, then the darkness I thought I had escaped would catch up to me. The all-too-familiar, chest-tightening, stomach-dropping, anxiety-inducing fear of what people thought would drag me back into insecurity and shame. I found myself so busy being the parts of myself I thought other people wanted that I couldn't possibly be whole. I gave everyone a piece until I had nothing left to hold on to.

My insecurities were magnified at my university because I began to rely more heavily on others to dispel my loneliness. The crazy thing is that, for the most part, I was able to make friends and join groups after those first few months but it was never enough. My loneliness never subsided because it wasn't about other people. I simply projected my own self-judgment onto others. My lack of authenticity created an echo chamber for my fears. Because I didn't know how to just be myself, I wasn't vulnerable enough to realize that others were facing the exact same struggles as me. I saw my lack of close friendships as confirmation that all my self-deprecating thoughts were true. Because I became insecure about my academics, I thought other people in my major must see me as dumb or wonder how I got there. Because I felt insecure about my personality, I thought other people viewed me as too serious or too corny or too stuck up. Eventually that kind of mentality slipped into every area of my life, particularly my appearance.

Freshman year, I wore clothes that were pretty revealing. I was raised in a household where a very strict standard of modest dressing was enforced so part of my reasoning was simply wanting to explore what I had never been allowed to do growing up. There was another reason though. To be completely transparent, I thought I was cute enough, but in order to get the attention I wanted, I had to dress a certain way. At eighteen years old, if someone tried to tell me that these were my motives, then I would have called them a liar and a hater. I would have said that I wore what I did because it made me look good and feel good. Sometimes that was the case, but sometimes, I simply wanted to be chosen. I didn't trust my opinion of myself, so even though I thought I looked good, I needed others— particularly men—to validate it before I believed it.

The twisted part is that no matter how many compliments or conversations I had, I could not cover my insecurity and self-consciousness. Although I was in constant need of affirmation, I couldn't possibly receive enough of it to love myself better, so my self-esteem plummeted. I have to emphasize it wasn't what I wore or said that took me away from God. Thinking about this in the wrong direction would lead to legalism. It was being far from God that caused me to behave in a way that didn't honor Him. Insecurity wasn't my sin. It was simply a tragic consequence of my imperfect humanity that caused me to sin. Before anything else, my sin was one of the heart and mind. My problem was much deeper than just revealing clothes. My sin was idolatry. I didn't know how to center God in my life, so I was bowing down at the altar of my insecurities. They had such a complete hold on me that I couldn't even recognize it. My insecurity was the most dangerous kind of enemy—the kind you allow to get close and grow unchecked because it looks like a friend.

I knew there had to be more. I remembered the joy-filled faces of the church people I'd grown up with all my life. If that was real, if God really made all the difference, then I wanted to give Him a fighting chance to heal me.

I tried to shake off the feeling that I'd never truly be happy or at peace, but those thoughts tormented me. I attempted to distract myself with schoolwork, various organizations, partying, and men. I only knew how to find my validation from external sources. They helped me feel okay for a while, but relief was always fleeting. When I was finally by myself again, the reality that I felt lost and alone came crashing back down on me. That cycle continued throughout freshman year as I sunk deeper into a horrible mental health spiral. I began to withdraw into myself more and more.

During the second semester of my freshman year of college, my depression got worse and I began to experience anxiety attacks. By then, I had painted such a confident persona that I was embarrassed by the idea of not loving myself as much as I claimed to. I was afraid to admit my struggles to others. But most of all, I was afraid to admit them to myself, because in some twisted way I thought that acknowledging my rapidly declining mental health would highlight some part of me that was actually less worthy of love. It was simply easier to pretend.

On some level, I felt that my insecurities were genuinely things I should hate about myself. I never consciously decided to adopt this mentality, though. It is only with the benefit of hindsight that I am able to clearly see what was happening. But at the time, I had a very "fake it till you make it" sort of attitude. I thought that if I projected the person I wanted people to see for long enough, then I would become her, and I could finally come out of hiding.

I didn't realize I was making myself unbearably lonely by making sure I was the only one who knew the real me, flaws and all. That early experience of shame and perversion deeply affected my ability to be vulnerable. I unknowingly sealed myself off, unable to understand my own identity, much less develop the capacity to share it with anyone else.

One night, toward the end of freshman year, I finally had enough. After struggling through a day of anxiety attacks and trying not to disturb my roommate with my quiet sobs, I was finally ready to surrender. I was tired of being in pain. I was fed up with the insanity of repeating the same cycles over and over. I had nowhere else to turn than the faith of my childhood. So, in my room, by myself, with no worship music playing or sermon to stir me up, I recommitted my life to Jesus. I promised to seek him for myself this time, not for my parents or anyone else. 2017 in my freshman dorm room was the first time I came to the end of myself, but it would not be the last. That night, I began to see Jesus as more than nice, I saw him as necessary. I took my anxiety, depression, and loneliness to the Cross. I took my people-pleasing and attention-seeking to the Cross. I took my identity to the Cross. That night marked the turning point in my relationship with God, but I still had a long way to go. The Bible says to pick up your cross daily, but I definitely skipped a few days on my journey back to faith.

...

Life got much brighter when I began to take my faith more seriously. When I sought God, He began to remind me who I was in Him and His light began to shine in my dim life; however, I still wasn't whole. It's important to realize that we can be in Christ and still be broken if we don't complete the process of unlearning. If we try to stack the Gospel on top of all our detrimental habits and ideas, we may end up saved without real healing taking place. Prayer works, but you can't just pray away the problem without the faith to do something about it. Why do you think there are so many Christians with world views that are against everything Jesus taught? Their spirits are saved, but their minds are not renewed.

After rededicating my life to Jesus, the anxiety and depression faded enough for me to function, but every so often I got this feeling that things weren't quite right. I was never really able to be consistent and committed to my relationship with God. I'd done everything I knew how to do. I was far from perfect, but when I said I was a Christian now, I knew what I meant and that was a big deal for me. However, it still felt like something was missing. I prayed and read my Bible more, but even though I began to develop a real and authentic relationship with Jesus, it was still so volatile and inconsistent. There were still so many insecurities in my life. I told God, "I'm really saved now. I'm trying to follow you. I feel like I should be better by now. I feel like I should be more whole by now."

By God's grace, as imperfect as I was, I stuck with my faith. Even if I couldn't feel it right away, I figured that loving Jesus more would help me love myself better. I didn't just want to cling to my family's religion anymore, I wanted to establish my relationship with God for myself. Part of it was because I believed in Him, but a larger part was because I wanted Him to make me feel better. Notice I said to *feel* better, not actually *be* better. I went to Jesus to fix my sadness and insecurity, but I still struggled with it. It made my relationship with God like an old, wooden roller coaster—unsteadily moving from one extreme to the other. My problem was that I didn't just need help from Jesus, I needed to embody him.

We tend to think that surrender is a moment, but in reality, it is a process. Surrender is a journey you embark on with God as He sanctifies you daily. As I pressed deeper

into God and surrendered more of my will for His, He
helped me realize I could deal with the symptoms of the
issue all day, but because I hadn't uprooted the
foundational idea that shaped my perception of myself and
groomed my insecurity for years, I would continue to
struggle with the same thing in Him as I did outside of
Him. Jesus was the answer, but my solution was specific.
Edward T. Welch says:

> As long as we are sinners, shame will be a familiar
> experience...The answer seems simple: Remember that
> in Jesus' death, resurrection, and ascension, through
> faith he has covered you with righteous robes, he has
> removed your shame. This might be the only teaching a
> fearful person needs. However...there are many times
> when a solution requires more than a reminder that
> Jesus died for us....I am not saying that the Gospel of
> Jesus is not enough. What I mean is that there are
> teachings implicit in the Gospel that need our
> attention.[11]

I had come into the house of the Lord, but there were
specific rooms that I needed to enter in order to really be

---

[11] Welch, Edward T. *When People Are Big and God Is Small.* P & R Publishing, 1997.

healed. Sometimes, when we genuinely come to Jesus and don't find ourselves immediately set free from all our issues, we make the mistake of thinking God isn't enough. The truth is, He's more than enough. We must ask ourselves: are we just coming to God, or have we allowed Him to come into us as well? I went to God to fix me, but I hadn't allowed Him to change me. I was just dealing with the symptoms, so I would never be able to fully eradicate the disease in my heart. When I realized that I would need to press deeper if I was ever going to be free, God began to change my desires so that I was desperate for more of Him. When I began to pray and meditate on the Word of God, He showed me my identity. He began to show me that the devil had twisted my personality and God-given gifts until I hated who I was divinely created to be.

The enemy rooted that deceit in the depths of my heart. Therefore, I naturally bore the fruit of shame and insecurity. Because I didn't know how to live out my God-given identity, I hid in the darkness. I had all this false humility that was rooted in prideful self-righteousness. Because I was so concerned with the way people saw me, I didn't have any room to be concerned about the people I saw. Because I was so worried about my perception of myself, I didn't have any space for how God perceived me. This led to cycles of depression, loneliness, and anxiety.

I have to confess that this cycle would have gone on forever if the divine grace of God hadn't reached out and interrupted me. God revealed to me that a lot of times we get saved and praise Jesus for our salvation, but if we are building the ideas and theology of the Christian life right on top of rotten foundations, then the trees of our lives will continue to bear bad fruit. Most people only see the pretty exterior of our fruits, but God knows that if you were to cut them open, they would be rotten on the inside. This is because we have roots that are corrupting His good seed, so we are unable to really reach the full potential God has for our lives. God has such a great vision and plan for us. He had so much He wanted to do for me and through me, but I was blocking my own ability to carry out His destiny for my life because I was content and complacent with my bad roots.

As I grew closer and closer to God throughout college, He slowly revealed my roots and transformed me through the Gospel. While I began to see the origins of my sinful behaviors, I also began to realize that those roots had become entangled in the depths of my life. But the question still remained—how could I uproot them?

. . .

The final turning point came at the end of my sophomore year of college. At my university, I was one of those people who knew a lot of people across campus and was involved in everything, but I was never really very close to anyone. I was very good at sharing just enough with friends so they felt like they knew me, even though deep down I knew they didn't. How could they when I barely knew myself?

Even as I'm writing this, I feel anxious about putting it out into the world because I'm not sure if I'm ready for others to see me clearly when I've only just begun to see myself. But I think if I had read something like this when I was younger, I wouldn't have felt so isolated in my feelings of inadequacy. I might not have cried so hard those nights when I was wondering what was wrong with me and why I didn't have close friends. I might not have felt so inexplicably trapped by how I wanted people—needed people—to see me. I might have developed an identity that was based on something more stable than my reflection in their eyes. Perhaps on that day when I laid my head against my tear-stained pillow at eighteen, I would have known what to do with the sudden, earth-shattering realization that I had no idea who I was outside of what I thought people wanted me to be. Perhaps during my freshman year of college, I could have behaved in a way that was true to myself and learned what I actually loved instead of tailoring my actions to the people whose approval I wanted.

But I didn't have anything like this book, so instead, I contorted myself into an unrecognizable shape in a desperate attempt to protect myself from the loneliness that had begun to leak out sporadically from all the cracks in my facade. If I had read something like this at that time, then perhaps instead of frantically trying to treat the seemingly unconnected symptoms of my sadness, I would have been able to diagnose the disease: an extreme case of Unknown Identity.

Since I didn't have a lot of guidance on what it meant to live a life that was fully committed to Jesus even after rededicating my life to him, I was still engaging in some pretty reckless behavior. I loved Jesus, but I was a young woman in college. I honestly just wanted to have a good time. I went to parties and kickbacks like everyone else, but my motives were wrong. I was searching for happiness, companionship, and belonging in superficial things. I'd been participating in some questionable sexual activities throughout college as a way to get validation and attention from men. But during sophomore year, in the spring of 2018, I went too far. Let's just say I did something I never thought I would do with a man I never thought I would do it with. There was alcohol and coercion involved, but it wasn't until much, much later that I understood it as a sexually abusive situation. At the end of the day, I made my decision that night and it took me to my lowest point yet.

Afterward, I took a shower in a desperate attempt to wash off the scent of regret that lingered on my skin. As the scalding hot drops of water slid over my body, I felt an overwhelming shame, unlike anything I'd ever experienced, come over me. It felt like a physical thing, on top of me, suffocating me, threatening to undo me. I couldn't escape it—the shame. I tried to scrub it off, but it was all over me, within me. I wanted to hide so badly, but how could I run away from myself? Once again, I felt like Eve in the garden—naked and ashamed of my sin. As I drowned in shame, it felt like the first time in a long time that I was finally able to see myself, and I looked incredibly...sad. I was a wilted, withered flower with only a faint memory of long-forgotten spring to hold on to. I sank to the floor of the shower and sobbed, my tears mixing with the water from the shower, mixing with my guilt.

Then I heard a voice clear as day—the voice of God. I heard Him tell me that I couldn't love myself because I didn't love Him. It seems like such a simple, obvious thing now, but at that moment the thought had actually never crossed my mind. There were things I was insecure about, and I dealt with loneliness and anxiety, but I thought I at least loved myself. I thought I was trying my best to love God, but I was so stubbornly proud that I couldn't even see how I was hurting myself by insisting that I could control my own life. Only God could have opened my eyes. He interrupted my shame and presented the Truth to me with no condemnation. Up until that moment, I understood self-hate as something that happened to other people, not me. Therefore, I suffered from it in the most detrimental way possible. I suffered in oblivion. I was someone with an open wound walking around casually like I wasn't about to bleed out at any moment.

James 1:23-24 (NIV) says, "Anyone who listens to the word but does not do what it says is like someone who looks at his face in a mirror and, after looking at himself, goes away and immediately forgets what he looks like." Yeah, unfortunately that was me.

At that point in college, I was an executive in my campus ministry, I had been a Christian all my life, I said I loved Jesus, and I went to church every Sunday. I might have had to drag myself out of bed in the morning after a drunken night, but I went. However, none of it mattered. Because all the while, I was trying to heal from the outside in. I followed the rules, but I did it so inconsistently and insincerely that I was no better than someone who didn't even try. I figured if I kept doing all the Christian things long enough, then I'd eventually become someone who could be committed, who didn't struggle so much to live for Christ.

I wanted to experience the supposed freedom that was in Christ, but because I didn't really know Him, see Him, or love Him, I was still bound to the sin He died for. I didn't want to be told what I could or couldn't do. My pride prevented me from seeing how truly broken I was. It stopped me from seeking the help I needed to get whole. It prevented me from having an intimate relationship with God. God couldn't gently tap me or redirect me with a quiet whisper. I wouldn't have listened. He loved me, so He let me exercise my free will. He let me crash and burn into an unrecognizable version of myself so I would finally become still enough to hear the Truth, and at that moment, the Truth set me free. The shame and guilt were not emotions from God. They were a human response to the Spirit of God in me that convicted me. He wasn't condemning me; He was inviting me to come back to Him. He wasn't pleased with my actions, but when I was at my lowest, God reminded me that nothing could separate me from His love. The Bible says:

Can anything ever separate us from Christ's love? Does it mean he no longer loves us if we have trouble or calamity, or are persecuted, or hungry, or destitute, or in danger, or threatened with death? . . . No, despite all these things, overwhelming victory is ours through Christ, who loved us. And I am convinced that nothing can ever separate us from God's love. Neither death nor life, neither angels nor demons, neither our fears for today nor our worries about tomorrow—not even the powers of hell can separate us from God's love. No power in the sky above or in the earth below—indeed, nothing in all creation will ever be able to separate us from the love of God that is revealed in Christ Jesus our Lord (Romans 8:35, 37-39 NLT).

Even at my lowest point, God loved the hell out of me. That night, on the floor of my shower, the realization of that Truth changed my life. The pivotal point didn't come when I figured out how to rid myself of shame or when I found my identity in the months after that painful night. It came right then when God showed me that, even after the worst thing I'd ever done, He still loved me more than I could even comprehend. That was the moment when I suddenly saw myself and my sin for what it was. But more importantly, I saw Jesus much more clearly. I wasn't distraught because my heart was broken, I was undone because God's heart was. And there I was with a hammer in one hand and blood on the other, staring him face-to-face, guilty of nailing him to the Cross all over again.

What I would come to discover later is that there are levels to freedom because there are levels to the truth. If the truth sets you free (John 8:32), then you can only be as free as the level of truth you're operating in. If there are undiscovered truths, then there is untapped freedom. Therefore, even though I accepted Jesus into my heart as a child, it wasn't until that miserable, tear-soaked moment in the shower that I was set free from the bondage of operating in the clutches of an unidentified condition. I was free from a hypocritical Christianity in which I daily crucified Jesus with my sin in private but then confessed to being his child in public. I was free to finally stop lying to everyone. But most importantly, I was free to stop lying to myself about the real condition of my heart. As the early morning darkness spread out over the world on that warm, spring night in 2018, through the shattered shards of my reality, I began to see the light.

- Six -

THE BREAKING POINT

I rest in my savior
The sorrow gives context for joy
Like a baby newly born into this world,
The hope stands as light
Against the backdrop of despair, I cried
Mourning the mistaken bliss of ignorance
Small and hungry
My growth limited by what I could see
A universe completely centered on my needs

After that fateful night, I went into my junior year of college. I faced incredible highs and tragic lows, but my focus shifted upward and inward. I was still very much a work in progress, but instead of trying to get attention from men, friends, and accomplishments, I began to lean into the presence of God. As I went through trials and difficult seasons, God revealed more and healed more. Life wasn't easy, but I had more joy than ever before. God surrounded me with the community I needed to keep me where He'd called me. I leaned into serving my campus ministry (shout out to Haven Student Fellowship) and found a home where there was enough grace and love for me to find a reprieve from the constant barrage of shame I was living under.

I'd been in this organization since I got to UT, but after that encounter sophomore year, I was committed to building my faith alongside other students with their own pains and struggles. With my Haven family, I discovered the Truth that I could anchor my life on. I found a relationship with God worth submitting to. As we celebrated testimonies and mourned tragedies together, this group became the physical embodiment of God's compassion towards me. I found a safe space where I could be vulnerable, but it was also a brave space that helped me find the courage to walk where God was calling me. Haven redefined what Christianity meant to me.

Over time, God began to reveal the answer to my question of how to uproot and unlearn the lies that had previously defined my character. I saw that the answer was

much simpler than I had imagined. I needed to redefine belief. My belief was broken. I was taught to know the Gospel, but I did not understand how to *believe* the Gospel—to believe it for myself, to believe that it is truth, and to allow it to radically redefine my life and show me my identity.

The Gospel was a thing that existed outside of me, but in order to overcome the mental attacks that I had been susceptible to, it needed to live within me. It needed to walk with me and talk with me. It needed to do more than just be something that I looked at and appreciated. It had to be something that I lived. I never made that my goal before, because I never knew it was the solution. I thought I *did* believe. I have so much love for my parents and teachers who planted seeds of faith in my young mind. But I watered those seeds sporadically, and unfortunately, due to a lack of understanding, my growth was stunted. I was told the truth at a very young age, but it didn't click. Like a misplaced puzzle piece, it just didn't fit, and so the picture of my life could never be completed.

However, the beautiful and divine part of this—which makes me fall to my knees and thank God—is that all these things still worked out exactly the way they were supposed to for my good. God didn't want me to make so many mistakes, but at the end of the day, He used my bad decisions for His glory. At the appointed time, not a moment too soon nor a moment too late, I ran into the life-altering presence of the Savior who had been there all along.

The experiences that I had in my adolescence and into college shaped me. Many of them left me feeling broken, fearful, lost, misunderstood, anxious, unheard, and sad. However, it was those very same experiences that made my encounter with Christ all the more transformational on that fateful night. I believe that I had encountered Jesus before. I was saved when I said the prayer at five years old, but I did not have the understanding to develop a lifestyle of faith. My belief didn't mature as rapidly as my age. When I came to the end of myself, it wasn't because of anything I did to deserve it. It was simply the grace of God. In His infinite mercy, God caused me to recognize my need for Him and the beauty of His Gospel. It was that Gospel of Jesus Christ that changed everything.

It is important to note that during this time, after the breakdown in sophomore year, I got better. But I still wasn't "fixed." God is not a mechanic. He doesn't just patch us up and send us on our way, expecting to see us again the next time we break down. God is more like a driver on the road to sanctification. He knows it is the journey of a lifetime, and if we are ready to stay in the passenger's seat and strap in for the ride, He'll lead us to our destination.

God helped me see that I'd been on that highway of faith since I'd accepted salvation as a young child. Sometimes I missed my exit or took a detour. Sometimes things got so bad that I hopped out of the car and started hitchhiking, so desperate to go somewhere that I was willing to ride along with anyone who stopped to notice me. But God was always there, both patiently waiting on me and mercifully redirecting me back to His love. By God's grace and divine timing, the moment He decided to completely reroute my destiny came when just about everything else around me became unfamiliar as well.

...

During the spring semester of my senior year of college, my world came to a stop as I stepped into the reality of a global pandemic. Like millions of people all over the world, I was forced to go into quarantine because I had been directly exposed to someone who tested positive for COVID-19. As I found myself alone, I knew that if I didn't use that period of far fewer excuses and far more time to seek the face of God, I would never have the opportunity again. During that season, even though I'd grown so much in my faith, the same cycles of loneliness, shame, and insecurity I'd been dealing with my entire life began bubbling up again, and I became desperate enough to demand a change. Something would have to give.

I said, "God forbid I come out of college just to be dealing with the same struggles I had when I got here." I wondered what would happen if I didn't just pray or study the Bible a bit more. I wondered what would happen if I took the time to focus exclusively on the Father, to make God my everything. I figured if there was a good time to lean into God, it was in the middle of quarantine when all my plans were canceled and God was literally the only person I could be close to.

I began to get curious about who I could be if I was really, completely sold out for Christ. I almost didn't believe it was possible. I mean, I wasn't a heathen; I loved Jesus. I just kind of figured I was as saved and spirit-filled as I was going to get. It had been two years since I chose the straight and narrow path in that shower. If God and I weren't besties by then, then I thought that level of relationship just might not be in the cards for us. But something about that idea just didn't sit right with me.

During that time, I was having a lot of strange dreams. I kept feeling convicted like God was trying to tell me something, but He was speaking a different language. I kept praying that God would show me what I should do, but I had no idea He'd respond by telling me who I should be.

That April of 2020, I went on a month-long media fast. I cut out anything that wasn't explicitly Christian—shows, movies, social media, books, music, even podcasts. I replaced these things with faith-based alternatives, so I was consuming more Godly content than I ever had in my life. I discovered a wealth of Christian content. However, the far more important thing was that I found myself in the presence of God more than I ever had in my life. I went on long prayer walks and read my Bible for hours, becoming increasingly sensitive in my spirit. On April 1st I wrote:

I just finished praying and God is impressing it on my heart so heavily that this is not a time for messing around. God's people are in desperate need of Him right now more than ever and they have not been equipped with the tools to seek Him for themselves. Therefore, it is our duty to be ministers of the Gospel. We need to share His divine abundance with His people. God's heart aches for His children, but He has already met their needs through us [his church]. Thank you Jesus.

This is a personal fast for clarity and purpose in my walk with God but this is also an intercessory fast for God's people who are suffering from this pandemic. It is for God to move in his divine power and love, cover his children in protection from corona and fear, and raise up his Church as a standard.

My prayers shifted from talking to God about myself to interceding on behalf of other people, and the funny thing is, the more I prayed for others, the more God began to reveal about myself. The more I pressed in, the more God began to uproot everything that He didn't plant in me. My anchor passage at that time was Ephesians 5:8-9 (NLT):

For once you were full of darkness, but now you have light from the Lord. So live as people of light! For this light within you produces only what is good and right and true.

I felt God drawing me closer and closer to Him, deeper into the light. Other than school, there were no distractions throughout my day to take my thoughts away from the Word of God. I was listening to sermons, reading books, and worshiping with music that was all Christ-centered, so it all reinforced what God was speaking to me through His

Word. I felt like I was reading the Bible for the first time, discovering the Gospel all over again. It was as if I'd always had my phone on low brightness in a dimly-lit room, and all of a sudden, someone turned the brightness all the way up and turned off the lights. I was consuming more light, but it appeared even brighter because I saw it in such stark contrast to all the darkness surrounding me.

The more the light of God was illuminated in my life, the more I was able to clearly see the darkness inside of me. The Word of God literally became a light unto my path and a lamp unto my feet (Psalm 119:105). I suddenly realized the lamp wasn't just necessary to get through the darkness of the world. The light of God first had to lead me out of the darkness that was within the depths of my own heart.

As the fast continued, I saw God use that time to reveal things about my past, my childhood, and my experiences that had been suppressed for so long that I had no idea they were at the root of some of my current, toxic thoughts. That month-long fast was the catalyst for the book you see before you today, because God showed me the connection between how I dealt with pornography in the books I was reading at a very young age and my skewed my idea of love and relationships. God showed me the depths of my prideful, selfish, people-pleasing, attention-seeking heart, and to put it lightly, I was shook. At first, I thought I was going into that fast so God could use me to help others, but the first person God needed to heal was me.

In those moments, it didn't feel like healing; it felt like brokenness and heartache. I cried...a lot. But every time, God was there. When I couldn't figure out how anyone but my momma had managed to love me, God was there, making me whole. He was there to speak life into me, to be my confidant and be my friend. He was there waiting to make a beautiful mosaic out of all my broken pieces.

At some point, I came to the realization that in the past—and even at the beginning of the fast—I went to God not because I thought He was all I needed, but because He was the only one there. Instead of wanting God for God, in some ways, I wanted Him because I couldn't get the relationships, attention, and satisfaction I really wanted from people and things. I was so infatuated with the creation that I had no room for the Creator. This realization truly humbled me, because even in that level of selfish pride, even when I sought Him for all the wrong reasons, God still showed up for me. He still chose to give me His pure, beautiful, reckless love when all I had to give Him was a tainted and fractured imitation.

It reminds me of the verse that says our righteousness is like filthy rags before God (Isaiah 64:6). He gave me everything I never even knew to ask for, and yet I was still unwilling and unable to trust such a trustworthy God with the depths of my brokenness.

I used to think I was so messed up that God wouldn't even look at me, but during this time, I understood that was a lie. I saw the character of God. God was never unable to look at me. I was saved, so He saw me just fine through the blood of Jesus. The truth was that I was unable to look at myself. How could I present myself fully to my God when I couldn't bear to see the full extent of my shame and depravity in comparison to His goodness? How could I see myself clearly when I couldn't see God clearly? If I really knew Him like I said I knew Him and loved Him how I said I loved Him, then I wouldn't be able to resist seeing the world through the filter of that love. I'd be able to love God's creation (including myself) so much that I could release the need to burden it with demands that can only be filled by a holy and righteous God. I discovered that I still had a long way to go, but there was so much grace in that. When I finally realized my problem, God could draw me close and actually develop me into the person He created me to be. God showed me that the solution wasn't to work even harder to prove I was good. Since I no longer operated from a place of shame, the answer came from letting go, giving up, and resting in the finished work of my Savior.

At some level, the fast brought me so close to God that I finally realized how far away I still was. That's why it was life-changing. I never really knew what it meant for someone to be radically transformed after only one encounter with Christ. I knew it was possible, but I'd never seen it in myself or anyone I knew. My transformation happened slowly at first, and then all at once. I think for people like me, who are born and raised in the church, the full manifestation of our faith tends to look a bit different from those who weren't. Although our hearts may decay on the same level, we know all the "right" things to do. Therefore, we may be more easily deceived into thinking that the conditions of our hearts are okay. At least that was the case for me.

I was saved for a long time, but during the process of that fast I finally started to get free. There were a lot of emotions in those vulnerable moments with God, but it was not the emotional response that allowed me to know I had encountered Jesus, it was what happened after I dried my eyes and got off of my knees. It wasn't about the feelings. It was a depth of knowledge and belief, a closeness to God that didn't just feel good to me, it was good for me. I sensed the mental weights I had been carrying my whole life falling off me. I didn't realize how deeply I'd still been struggling with shame until God set me free.

The interesting thing was that the negative thoughts didn't just disappear. I didn't just become fearless in that single moment. There was no magic to it. Nothing in my life actually changed except for my perspective. I was much more clearly able to distinguish the Truth from the lies. I was able to look at my insecurities about my acne and lack of close friends, my concern about what people were thinking about me, and my anxiety about the future for what they were—symptoms of pride, shame, fear, and unbelief. They lost the power to define me. For the first time, I was able to see these emotions objectively without allowing them to control me and determine my reactions. I was able to see them clearly enough to hand them over to God without clinging to the familiarity of my brokenness. I was free to find joy because I got the chance to rest in the arms of my Father while He fought those battles I was too weary to engage in.

This was my process of uprooting. It changed me in so many ways, but at the same time, I never felt more like myself. When I leaned into faith through that time of fasting, God allowed me to experience His presence in a way that radically shifted how I saw God, then myself, and then others. He turned on the lights and began to uproot all the lies that had entangled my heart in darkness for so long.

Without all the self-focused thoughts about what I was not and what I should be taking up so much mental real estate, I was free to focus on God's purpose for my life. I was able to love myself because I knew God's love for me. I realized that if He says I'm worthy of His love, then who am I to argue? Do I know more than the God who made me?

Seeing God clearly gave me the confidence to know that I can find joy even when I don't have control. It helped me to love other people as image-bearers as well. It seems so simple, but I finally realized that other people are so much more than what they can do for me. I do not have any ownership over their lives or entitlement to their love, only God has that. No one owes me acceptance or admiration or friendship. I cannot be entitled to another image-bearer. My job is to love them, not use them. Please understand that people didn't send you here, so people can't stop you. Your life is so much more important than the approval or rejection of man.

Contrary to popular belief, this thinking won't cause you to isolate yourself or cut people off. It will empower you to love others better. Focusing on God more and yourself less makes you secure enough to care for others and show unconditional love, because you do not need reciprocation in order to know that you are valuable and worthy. You can then have relationships that are more meaningful, because your love for other people isn't centered on you; it is centered on God. His love simply flows through you and to others. You never run out because your source is infinite. You are not a pond—a dumping ground for the good and bad opinions of others. You are a pipe—a vessel that opinions can flow through and flow to while it remains connected to an everlasting source, a love powerful enough to wash away every insecurity—the living water of God.

When I didn't love God, I didn't have enough energy to properly love my neighbor as myself like the Bible commands because I was constantly filtering everything through the lens of ME. How will they see ME? What will they think of ME? What if they reject ME? People who are deeply insecure like I was find themselves in a paradoxical position because they spend a lot of time thinking about others but never consider other people for their own sakes. The other person is always a means to an end. The end is always centered on what you need. You find yourself in a toxic cycle of people-pleasing, so even when you are kind or go out of your way for someone, it's usually more about how that action makes *you* look or makes *you* feel. That's no way to show genuine, authentic love. That's not how God shows love. God doesn't love us because He gets anything out of it. He loves us purely for our benefit. God is full and complete in and of Himself. He has no need for us to affirm Him or praise Him. Our worship simply makes Him glad. Because He is a perfectly secure God, He loves us from a selfless place. He is Love and His love is perfect (1 John 4), which is why He must be our source.

When you're loving someone—even yourself—from an insecure place, you love them pridefully. Remember that, sometimes, pride is thinking too much of yourself. But other times, pride is thinking of yourself too much. Attempting to love yourself out of pride is loving yourself for what you can do and who you can be rather than who you are in Christ. Attempting to love someone else from a place of pride is loving them for what they can do for you and who they can be for you instead of who God created them to be. We were not designed to constantly be our own focus; we were designed to use our minds and every other part of our lives to glorify God. Therefore, deep insecurity hinders your ability to live a life that glorifies God.

Once I understood the roots of my insecurity and self-hate, I saw that I needed to focus on God until He was the only thing in my view. I needed to seek after Him until I had no choice but to see the whole world through Christ-colored lenses. I would have to do the hard work of unlearning years of fear, shame, and pride, but I would start by fixing my eyes on Jesus, the author and finisher of my faith. Through him, everything can be seen so much more clearly, because God is light and He illuminates our lives.

The beautiful thing about Jesus is that his yoke is easy and his burden is light (Matthew 11:28-30). There is an active role we need to play in submitting to Jesus daily. It is not always easy, but we don't have to struggle to fix ourselves. When God begins to do the work, He simply points to the broken pieces so we're clear on exactly what we need to surrender. In Psalm 139:23 (NIV), the Bible says, "Search me, God, and know my heart; test me and know my anxious thoughts."

What we must understand is that we don't have to invite God into the messy depths of our hearts for Him to see what is there. He knows our hearts already, so we invite Him into our hearts for our own sakes. We are the ones who need to confront the darkness deep within. By asking God to search our hearts, the intention must be to discover a faulty mindset, motive, or heart-posture so we can consciously surrender it to God.

The idea is not so different from a therapist linking your current behavior to something you suppressed from your childhood. You have lived your life, you are familiar with your own experiences, and yet there is something deeper that needs to be brought to the light in order for you to move forward from the toxic cycles that have bound you.

However, God is so much more than a therapist. He created the heart that He's searching, so He knows exactly what to look for and how to heal it. Now don't get me wrong—I love therapy. I think God can use a therapist to get you through this process of heart work and uprooting. You can even get very helpful strategies to heal. But because God is God, He is the only one who can make you whole again. He's the one who will return you back to the way He created you, regardless of what you've been through. He can guide you to the point where you're ready to confront the darkest parts of your heart and let God's light shine through. When you take time to retreat and sincerely seek the face of God, He will make Himself known to you. It is in that place where the light shines so brightly that darkness has no home—it is there we find wholeness in Christ. I like to call that place the Light Point.

- *Seven* -

LIVING IN THE LIGHT

My weeping was forgotten in the prison of night
Now I am free I know the light
of the morning
To fully form was to be exposed
Naked and unafraid
Like Eve before the fall
I see the fruit of life
Unbound by shame

y journey has been a process of learning how to live in the light. Living in the light simply means having the freedom to walk boldly and honestly while serving others with your God-given purpose and identity. The light is a place in Christ where you are free from fear and shame. Living in the light comes out of a life that has been transformed by a close and personal relationship with your Creator. It is not a life in which there is no hurt or pain. In fact, the process of coming into the light might be a painful one. But, more often than not, our purpose is connected to our pain.

My story is one of overcoming deep shame, fear, and insecurity, but it's bigger than me. My story isn't significant because I am particularly important or influential. My story matters because it was divinely orchestrated by my Creator. If I had not known darkness, I could never really understand the light. Light refuses to be contained. It spreads like wildfire, setting everything in its path ablaze. It is eager to be shared. It yearns to be invited in. It makes its presence known, but it will not force you to accept it.

Have you ever had someone turn on a bright light after your eyes had adjusted to a very dark room or when you were in the middle of deep sleep? Your natural instinct is to shut your eyes and retreat. Unless you expect the light, unless you choose it intentionally, you are far more likely to prefer the comfortable familiarity of the darkness.

Outside of God, darkness is our natural habitat. We are born in it, raised in it, and trained by it. It seeps into every crack and crevice of our minds. In the dim environment of our fallen world, that which is evil looks appealing and that which is good and holy appears undesirable. In the darkness, lies are mistaken for truth and fear seems far more powerful than faith. In the darkness, we are doomed to repeat toxic cycles and destructive patterns, because although we know better, we can't seem to do better no matter how hard we try.

In 1 Peter 2:9 (NIV), The Bible says: "But you are a chosen people, a royal priesthood, a holy nation, God's special possession, that you may declare the praises of him who called you out of darkness into his wonderful light."

God is an infinitely loving and patient Father. He's a gentleman. He doesn't force you into the light or drag you, kicking and screaming, into His presence. He knows that any step taken outside of free will will eventually send you running back to the darkness. Your sinful nature may have caused you to dwell in darkness, but God created you to be a light-walker. God is Light, and He sent His Son to die so He could adopt us into His illuminated family.

When Peter says that we have been called out of the darkness and into His wonderful light, he is saying that God called us unto Himself. It's one thing to be called, but it's an entirely different thing to answer the call. God is Light. He's holding out His hand to invite you into communion with Himself. The question is, will you answer the call?

Many are chosen, few are called, but even fewer actually answer the call to step out of the darkness and into the light. God sets life and death before us (Deuteronomy 30:15). He encourages, instructs, and motivates us to choose life—to choose light. He desperately wants you to make the right choice. He wants it so badly that He paid the ultimate sacrifice, just so you could have the chance to enter into His presence. But God loves us too much to force us to love Him back. Accepting Jesus Christ as your Lord and Savior is the first step to living in the light. But unfortunately for so many Christians, it is also the last step. There are many who believe in Jesus but are still living in the shadows. Their souls are saved, but they don't understand the freedom they have been given. Just because you have accepted your invitation into God's family doesn't mean you are aware of His presence. It's not enough to just step out of the darkness, you must also step into the light.

When I got saved, I didn't understand how to walk in God's marvelous light. Like many new Christians, I thought the prayer of salvation was the climax of my faith story when it was really just an introductory paragraph. Because I believed in Jesus, I had hope in the light, but I was not yet living in it. What I thought was the full illumination of God's presence was really just a candle. I had gotten just enough of God to light a little candle, and I had it right in front of my face, so a small circle around me was illuminated. But I couldn't see into the distance. I had no vision for what God could do in my life. I was no longer in complete darkness, but it was...dim.

Beyond the confines of my small circle of light lay my purpose, my identity, the relationships God wanted me to build, and my potential to impact the world through His love. And there I was, unable to even visualize my next step of faith because my vision was stunted. Like someone who fumbles around a house in the dead of night with only the memory of daytime to guide their path, I had come home to Christ, but what should have been comfortable had become unfamiliar because I'd grown so accustomed to the darkness. At times, I tried to reach beyond myself and explore what was out of sight, but I stumbled around in trepidation and was unable to move freely due to fear of what might be lurking in the shadows.

Afraid of tripping and falling over unseen obstacles, I felt around with restricted movements. I could see myself, but I could not see what was beyond me. Therefore, I was not free. I think a lot of us are like that—content to live in the dimly-lit confines of our self-centered Christianity, delivered from some sins, but also tiptoeing timidly around our callings because we haven't taken that step of faith into the light. When you are in that small circle of light, you only have enough sight for yourself. Those around you appear dimly lit as well. Even God appears less magnificent than He should because the small light—the limited truth and freedom you've accepted—has led to a wrong perspective on Him and His creations.

There is infinite space to stretch out and explore in the presence of God, but when we live outside the light, we confine ourselves to cramped corners instead. Imagine the freedom with which you might run through a big open field in the middle of the day. Your vision doesn't go on forever, but you can see far enough to move with confidence. You are not running away from anything; you are running towards the light. You feel the soft jade blades of grass under your feet and the brilliant rays of golden sunshine beaming down on your flushed cheeks. You are running towards God's destiny for your life. Because God is immense, you are seeking Him and in His presence all at once. He is all around you. He surrounds you with His glory. Because you have accepted the invitation into the light, that moment is on Earth as it is in Heaven.

That choice to go deeper into the presence of God is the difference between secrecy and transparency, between lies and truth, between sadness and joy. It is the difference between living in the dark and thriving in the light.

. . .

In James, the Bible speaks of God as "…the Father of the heavenly lights, who does not change like shifting shadows" (James 1:17 NIV). So many of us are stuck living in the shadows, with parts of our lives illuminated by the glory of God on the surface while the other, deeper parts are still cloaked in darkness. But life in the shadows can be deceptive. Shadows have a way of distorting reality to make things appear bigger and more frightening than they really are. In the shadows, it's very easy to conceal the truth.

Living in the light of God is not a subtle experience. This is the Creator of the universe we're talking about; His presence is revolutionary. It is the same light that guided the Israelites through the wilderness and blinded Paul on the way to Damascus. The light of God is life-changing. It is one thing to say you believe in Jesus, but it is an entirely different thing to have him be the light of your life—a constant guide who illuminates every step. It's okay to start in the shadows, but oftentimes as Christians, we get stuck there, afraid to let go and fully embrace the light of God. After all, in God's light, there is nowhere to hide. It can feel like you are exposed and vulnerable. In the light, you have nothing to lean on but God. So you have to surrender to someone you can't see. The process of learning to trust that His glory can carry the full weight of your brokenness is challenging, but it's necessary to live freely.

I found true freedom in faith when I discovered intimacy in the light of God. The Bible is full of references to the idea that the Gospel sets us free, including 2 Corinthians 3:17, Galatians 5:1, and John 8:32.

"Then you will know the truth, and the truth will set you free."

John 8:32 (NIV)

But just because you've been set free doesn't mean that you live freely. Claiming Christianity without experiencing freedom is like being in a cage with an open door and refusing to walk out. If the door is unlocked but you never take the steps to actually walk out of it, then practically, you are no better than the person who is shackled in.

This was the problem that the Children of Israel faced. God delivered them and brought them out of the bondage of slavery in Egypt, but when they faced challenges, they defaulted back to a slave mentality. In Numbers 14:3-4

(ESV), after the Israelites had just been delivered out of bondage in Egypt, they began to complain and say:

> 'Why is the Lord bringing us into this land, to fall by the sword? Our wives and our little ones will become prey. Would it not be better for us to go back to Egypt?' And they said to one another, 'Let us choose a leader and go back to Egypt.'

Their bodies were out of captivity, but their minds couldn't understand that familiar wasn't better than free.

Many people confuse deliverance with freedom. In his sermon, *Cravings of the Wilderness,* Pastor Jerry Flowers defines deliverance as a state where you have been relocated even if your mind hasn't caught up yet. He defines freedom as a state where your mind has been relocated even if your place hasn't caught up yet.

The praise that Paul and Silas were able to give in a jail cell was only possible because their minds and spirits had been set free by God. Their freedom wasn't determined by the situation they found themselves in. Their freedom came from absolute knowledge of the Truth. They didn't just believe in an idea of the truth; they had a relationship with the Truth because they were in intimate communion with God.

In contrast, God brought the Israelites out of Egypt, but it took an entire generation for their minds to catch up to the reality of their new position. They were delivered after they crossed the Red Sea, but they were not free until forty years later when they reached the Promised Land. God brought them out of the darkness, but because the darkness was still in them, they behaved from a place of bondage and were stuck in the wilderness for far longer than necessary.

Deliverance is something you receive without much effort on your part. Jesus did all the work to secure your deliverance when he died on the cross to overcome death, hell, and the grave. When someone is delivered, they are rescued from danger or harm. In this way, the free gift of salvation was an act of deliverance. We were lost in sin and death, and God delivered us out of darkness into his kingdom (Colossians 1:13). However, just because you are delivered doesn't mean you are free. While deliverance takes no effort on your part other than belief, freedom has a condition. Freedom is predicated on knowledge of the Truth. You shall know the Truth, and *then* you shall be free.

If you've been freed but you don't understand the Truth of how to walk in that freedom, then you're not really free at all. If this idea confuses you, don't worry—the disciples were confused too. In John 8, they asked Jesus how they could be made free if they were never enslaved in the first place. Jesus responds by explaining the difference between physical and spiritual enslavement. He goes on to say that whoever commits sin is a slave to sin, but who the Son sets free is free indeed (John 8:34-36 NIV). While we have all sinned and fallen short of the glory of God (Romans 3:23), the hope of life in Christ is that we might be empowered through the Holy Spirit to live a life that is free of sin. This is not a life that is perfect; it is simply a life that is perfectly submitted to God.

You might think you are already free; however, if you keep repeating the same "small sins," if you keep falling victim to overwhelming anxiety and fear, if you are stuck in a cycle of succumbing to sexual temptations, if your faith is so lukewarm that you practice people-pleasing, perfectionism, and pride on a regular basis, then please believe me when I say that you are not yet as free as you can be. Although you have probably heard some truths, you do not yet know *the* Truth, and therefore, you are not walking in the fullness of the freedom that Jesus died for.

What you must understand about freedom is that it is not a place you arrive at, but it is a journey you embark on. Complete freedom will only come when we enter into glory, but there is a kind of freedom you can walk in during your time here on Earth as well. That freedom is found in not just knowing *about* the Truth but knowing *the* Truth. It is found in not just knowing about Christ but knowing Christ personally. After all, Jesus is the way, the Truth, and the life. To know him is to know Truth. When you know Truth (God) for yourself, then you can have a personal, intimate relationship with it. The more you allow it to become a part of you, the more you will be able to walk in the freedom that comes from it.

Too many people who claim the label of Christianity are walking in bondage right alongside those who don't believe. Although they love God in theory, they don't know Him practically. Christianity is not about religious rules and regulations; it is about a person—Jesus Christ—stepping into humanity so that our souls may be saved from the death we deserve, because of our sins. Christianity is about redemption and restoration into a right relationship with the Heavenly Father. Many Christians stop at accepting this Truth in our heads and never let it seep into the depths of our hearts. We limit our understanding of God to what He can do for us instead of expanding it to who He is to us.

It is quite possible to live saved while staying bound. That was my experience. I was bound in shame and insecurity even though I believed in Jesus Christ. I was stuck in the same cycles of sin and guilt, even though I was saved and I thought I loved God. Why? Because I didn't know how to grab hold of what God had already given me access to. When your spirit is free but your mind is still in bondage, then you live far below God's good will and plan for your life.

Jesus said that his yoke is easy and his burden is light (Matthew 11:28-30). But I was so fearful and desperate to manage my own struggles that I never accepted the rest that could only come when I reached the end of myself and surrendered my mind, body, and soul to the one who created it.

It breaks my heart that so many young Christians have entered the compound of faith but they don't see the value of entering the house of the Lord. They prefer to lounge outside on the patio of the Father's mansion. They love to have the waiters attend to them and enjoy the picturesque views, but they never allow themselves to grow curious about what lies beyond the door of the house. Going inside would require them to exert themselves and be uncomfortable. So they stay where they are, denying themselves access to the Father.

On the other side of that door is peace and joy in the Holy Spirit. On the other side is freedom from addiction, perversion, and insecurity. On the other side is the purpose God put them on the Earth to accomplish. The door is unlocked; they've been invited in. All they have to do is turn the knob and walk into the light. There they will find a God-given inheritance. They have the opportunity to enter the living room, sit down with the owner, and discover how magnificent it is to be in His presence rather than just on His property. But they remain outside, stuck on their Father's land without all the good things He's prepared for them, simply because they will not open the door. They don't understand the access they've been granted. They are held back by fear, self-condemnation, or ignorance.

Like the older brother in the story of the prodigal son, they've been invited into the feast of freedom in the house of the Lord, but they stay outside, close enough to smell the joy but too far away to experience it. If this describes your experience with God, then this book is an invitation to take a step forward and walk into the life that Jesus died for you to live.

I believe that this is one reason why more and more people are leaving the faith. You can be saved without an intimate relationship with God, but that's not all He wants for us. Deliverance can bring you into the faith, but freedom will keep you there. When God becomes more real to you than anything else, when you begin to love Him for who He is to you and not just what He can do or what you've heard about Him, when you discover that the darkness of the world can't hold a candle to the beautiful light of Christ, *that* is when following Jesus becomes irresistible. We will never find the joy and peace of salvation in Christ unless we learn how to let go of whatever it is that we cling to more tightly than God.

What do you need to let go of so that your hands will be free to open that door to your Father's house?

The beautiful thing is that you only need one free hand to open that door, because as grace would have it, God doesn't need you to have everything together before He welcomes you home. He just needs a step of faith in the direction of the light. In your other hand, you may still be holding on to hurt, pain, and shame, and that's okay. God says you can come into the house with those things. In fact, He wants you to, because God's home is not for those who think they can get healed on their own; it's for those who know they can't.

I want you to do more than just read my story. I want you to understand that the only way to live in the light is to develop an intimate, vulnerable relationship with the Savior of your soul. Understand that God wants to give you so much more than surface-level Christianity. I know you may never have heard it this way before, but please listen to me when I say that if God's only purpose for your life was to save your soul, then He would have called you up to glory the moment you believed in Jesus Christ. If all He cared about was your eternal destiny, then why would He leave you here on Earth where there are endless opportunities to fall back into sin and reject the free gift of salvation?

We say we're saved. So what? What implications does that have for us right now? Why does your faith matter if our lives look no different and our struggles have no more meaning than those who don't know Christ? Salvation happens the moment we give our lives to Jesus, but it is also happening in every moment after that as he makes us more like him. And it will happen once and for all when we see him in glory. It is both the motivation for our faith and the destination of our faith. Unless we begin to see salvation as both the endgame and the starting point, we will be trapped in the sad reality of way too many people who know Christianity but don't know Christ.

. . .

You are here for a purpose. God has good works that He's destined for you before you were even born (Ephesians

2:10), and He also knows the person He created you to be. His will is not for you to be trapped in a cycle of shame and insecurity. His will is not for you to be living in fear and mistaken identity. His will is for you to be free. If there is one thing I've learned, it is that we don't get free in the dark. Freedom is only found when you step out into the light. This is not just my opinion; it is a biblical truth. The Bible says in John 14:6 (NIV), "I am the way and the truth and the life. No one comes to the Father except through me." So if God is Truth and the Truth will set you free, then that means God will set you free. But Truth can only set you free if you know it.

So here are my questions for you: Do you know the Truth? Do you know God? I mean, do you *really* know Him? You may know *about* Him, but do you know who He is to you personally? Do you have a close, intimate relationship with your Lord and Savior who died to give you that opportunity?

I believe so many of us live in the shadows of our mistakes instead of in freedom because, although we may practice Christianity, we don't really know Christ. What I had to realize after dealing with the insecurity and shame that controlled my life for years was that my life wouldn't change from just being in proximity to God. I needed to get closer. If I was ever going to experience the joy of His salvation instead of constantly falling back into old patterns and trying to claw my way back into God's presence, then something would have to change.

If you're reading this and thinking, "Oh yeah, that's good advice for the baby Christians, but God and I go all the way back. He knows I know Him," then maybe you should reexamine your heart—none of us can even begin to comprehend the depths of an infinite God and we fool ourselves when we believe we have all the knowledge of Him that we need.

If I had kept on going down the same trajectory of faith, without choosing to know the God who made the ultimate sacrifice on the off-chance that I would choose Him back, then I would always find Christianity but I would never find Christ. There is value in religion, but I think that when you encounter religion before you encounter Christ, then it can distort the experience of God so much that the love which should draw you in becomes fear that pushes you away.

It is not enough to have one encounter with God; we must experience Him consistently. If your encounter fades as soon as your environment changes, then you may have been convicted for the moment but you weren't convinced for the journey. So many of us come to God because of a feeling. We stay with God as long as we have that feeling, but then the feeling fades and we think God is fading with it. But you were never supposed to focus on the feeling; you were supposed to focus on the Father.

God allowed me to get to a place where I was desperate for Him. In a time of prayer and fasting, I cried out to Him and He met me right where I was. He intentionally taught me how to build intimacy with Him. When I expressed my desire to really know God, He not only revealed Himself to me, but He also showed me how anyone who desires to be free and grow in intimacy with the Father can do so. My journey from darkness to light wasn't just for me, so I'd be doing you a huge disservice if I shared my testimony without also sharing my process. Developing intimacy with God is the way we come to live in the light. I had no idea how to do it until the Holy Spirit took me by the hand and showed me. The first step was understanding what intimacy means and why it is necessary.

Living in the Light

Eight

AN INTIMATE GOSPEL

Basking in love
Born again into the light of day
With nowhere to hide
All the imperfections magnified
But out here I can…breathe
My heart beating, my soul singing free
From the death that once defined me
Loved, By God, To death,
In death and back to life again

he Gospel changes everything. The Gospel is the Good News that God sent His only Son—Jesus—to enter into human history, live a perfect life, die for our sins, and rise to life again. He did this by grace alone so that we (the whole world) could be saved from judgement and restored back to a right relationship with God. If we believe by faith in the finished work of salvation and confess our sins, then we will be saved (Romans 10:9). This truth is revolutionary and life-changing. It is the only thing that was powerful enough to rescue me from the bondage of sin and shame, but even more than that, the Gospel is beautiful. It is not about what I can do; it is about what Jesus has already done.

The heart of the Gospel is not a religious text or even an idea. At the heart of the Gospel is a person. Therefore, the Gospel isn't just something you look at; it is a reality you live out daily, empowered by Jesus Christ. The Gospel is eternal but it is also personal. The power and love of Jesus Christ working in me has led me out of the darkness and into the glorious light of God. However, just like any relationship, there are ways that our relationships with Christ can grow and deepen.

I wish that, when I was younger, someone would have helped me understand that coming to Jesus doesn't just secure your eternal destiny, but it guarantees your earthly freedom as well. God's goodness is unchanging, no matter what stage of relationship you find yourself in right now. Whether you can feel Him right beside you, or He seems so distant you're not even sure if He exists, God is still good and His love for you is infinite.

God loves everyone, but it is important to accept Jesus as your Lord and Savior in order to join the family of faith. Whether you've already accepted salvation, or you might in the future, please understand that saying the prayer of salvation is a starting point. It is the moment when you are justified—set free from the penalty of your sins through the death of Jesus on the cross. However, salvation is more than just that moment. It is a life-long journey in which you were saved, you are being saved, and you will be saved.

Please realize that salvation means you now have access to the incomparably perfect God of the universe. Do not underestimate the magnitude and significance of that. Salvation begins a process of sanctification where the power of the Holy Spirit sets us free from sin and gives us the power and desire to do what pleases God (Philippians 2:13). Through sanctification, we are being saved from the power that sin once had over our lives. When our time on Earth is done and we see Jesus, face-to-face, as Christians, we have the hope that we will be saved from the presence of sin. This is known as glorification.

Let me be real with y'all. I didn't get a full picture of the Gospel when I first said the prayer of salvation and accepted Jesus into my heart. I pretty much stopped at

John 3:16. Maybe it's just me, but I really thought that some people just did the most when they found Jesus and others didn't. I thought salvation had more to do with the moment of prayer than the lifestyle that followed it. The concept of a continuous sanctification process was never taught to me. Or if it was, it didn't resonate at all. If I'm being honest, it took years of suffering and sadness after giving my life to Jesus before I realized I had missed something along the way. I'd grown up believing that my Christianity was basically built into my DNA. I'm eternally grateful that my parents planted the seeds of faith in my life. It helped me to believe in the *idea* of Jesus, but the practical reality of *choosing* him as not only Savior, but also Lord—the ruler, master, and king over my life—was a different story entirely.

I said I gave my life to Jesus—I believed I gave my life to Jesus—but for someone who claimed to have the light, I was still living in so much darkness. I didn't understand that my relationship with Christ should change my whole life, so I struggled with the condemnation that Jesus had already delivered me from (Romans 8:1). I didn't realize that salvation should lead to transformation, not because I had to follow a bunch of religious rules, but because I would experience the beauty of Love and I would desperately want to be like Him. I didn't know that it was the power of the Holy Spirit working in me that would then empower me to live like Jesus.

For a long time, I was clinging on to the attitudes, behaviors, and desires of "the world." Not everything secular is horrible, but I had no basis for discerning the distracting from the dangerous because my fundamental worldview wasn't based on Christ. It was based on what felt good, what looked good, and what other people told me was good. I got just enough of God to feel saved, but I didn't give Him enough of me to actually live a transformed life.

Even after giving my life to Jesus at a very young age, I tiptoed the line between Christianity and my own desires because I still wanted to have fun. I think that's the case with a lot of young Christians, especially those of us who grew up in Church. We think Jesus is cool and all. He can have Sunday mornings and even the five minutes it takes me to read my devotion every day. But I need *my* friends, *my* fun, *my* goals, *my* resources, *my* trauma, and *my* sexuality. Jesus can have whatever is left. At least that's how I felt. The choice I was given of God vs. "the world" simply didn't match up with my reality. I grew up hearing that I should be in the world but not of the world, but that distinction of us vs. them never felt right to me. The separation in my life was more like what I wanted and felt like doing vs. what God said I was supposed to be doing.

When serving Jesus felt good or scratched that people-pleasing itch I had, then I was cool with it. But as soon as it cost me something and as soon as I had to give up control, I tried to snatch back the life I'd given to Jesus faster than you could say, "Won't he do it!" I held on to so much that I needed to let go of in order to be more like Christ. I didn't realize that by clinging so hard to the enjoyment I thought I had outside of His will, I was denying myself the joy of His presence. Instead of actually trying to be like Christ, I was trying to be like a Christian. I was following a western, cultural, unbiblical model of Christianity and expecting to look like a holy, counter-cultural, truth-filled Christ.

Like most of you reading this, I had the best intentions, but it was never going to work. Really think about the phrase "giving your life to Jesus." When you get saved, you acknowledge that your life is not your own. You give it away because you realize it belongs to someone else. I was not made for myself. Therefore, all those years I was claiming Christianity, I was confused because I wasn't actually following Christ. It wasn't about my actions, it was about my heart. I'd created a version of my faith that didn't require me to change my life in any drastic way. The Gospel is revolutionary. I may have turned about twenty degrees, but there was definitely no revolution in my life. I thought I was serving the God of the Bible who made me in His image, but I was really serving a God of my own creation who I'd made in my own image. I was serving a God who never disagreed with me, never challenged me, and never made me do anything that I didn't feel like doing. I had my reasons and excuses, but at the end of the day, I was serving myself. I had become my own god because I didn't believe in the true God enough to surrender.

. . .

My greatest downfall wasn't my addiction to sexual content, pride, fear, or even disobedience. At the end of the day, my fundamental sin was unbelief. Jackie Hill Perry says this of unbelief:

Unbelief doesn't see God as the ultimate good. So it can't see sin as the ultimate evil. It instead sees sin as a good thing and thus God's commands as a stumbling block to joy. In believing the devil, I didn't need a pentagram pendant to wear, neither did I need to memorize a hex or two. All I had to do was trust myself more than God's Word. I had to believe that my thoughts, my affections, my rights, my wishes, were worthy of absolute obedience and that in laying prostrate before the flimsy throne I'd made for myself, that I'd be doing a good thing.[12]

Even after I said the prayer of salvation, it took me a long time to believe that the Good News was actually good for me. In an attempt to accept something I didn't fully understand, I became something that grieves God's heart even more than a heathen—a hypocrite (Revelations 3:15-16). I knew all the right things to say and do in order to appear Christian in front of the people who cared about that sort of thing, but I didn't really love God. I wasn't intentionally trying to be deceptive, but I didn't see Him and didn't know Him, so I *couldn't* love Him. You must understand that for someone who doesn't know her identity, it is perfectly natural to be a different person in front of different people. The version I presented at any given time felt authentic to me, but even my understanding of authenticity was wrong. I was walking around with so many fractured pieces of myself, I had no idea how to

---

[12] Perry, Jackie Hill. *Gay Girl, Good God.* B&H Books, 2018.

present all of myself to God. When you are not anchored in the Truth and you don't have an objective standard of good and evil, you think everything that looks good and feels good is good.

Tim Keller says it like this:

If you pick and choose what you want to believe and reject the rest, how will you ever have a God who can contradict you? You won't! You'll have...A God, essentially, of your own making, and not a God with whom you can have a relationship and genuine interaction. Only if your God can say things that outrage you and make you struggle (as in a real friendship or marriage!) will you know that you have gotten hold of a real God and not a figment of your imagination.[13]

I wanted to be a Christian but still do things my way. So instead of deferring to God's authority, I tried to claim the label of Christianity without the responsibility of being a Christ-follower. It felt good to impress people, to try and be the person they expected. It felt good to pick and choose a version of faith that never required me to really look at

---

[13] Keller, Timothy. *The Reason for God: Belief in an Age of Skepticism.* Penguin Books, 2008, pp. 113-114.

myself and admit the desperate wickedness of my heart. It felt good to use alcohol and accolades to numb my pain. I didn't know who I was, and the parts I did know, I didn't like, so it felt good to be someone else. It all felt good...until it didn't.

At some point, the crushing weight of trying to be everything to everybody and feeling like I was nothing to anybody simply became too much to bear. This happened years after I'd come to Jesus, but it was the exact moment I allowed his love to come to me. God, in His loving grace and tender mercy, reached down past my pain and helped me fully believe. He didn't just intellectually help me believe that Jesus was the Son of God who died and rose again. I believed that when I was saved at five years old. By His divine grace and mercy, which I still can't comprehend, God changed my heart and showed me that the implications of this Truth should radically transform the way I lived my life. He empowered me to drag all my baggage into the light. He helped me see that the Truth of the Gospel really is powerful enough to make me whole. I saw that the Gospel is the good news because it is about a good God, and that simple reality changes everything.

The most amazing thing about God is that He can use someone as hurt and rebellious and imperfect as me to proclaim His intimate Gospel to a lost world. God is using the very story I thought would disqualify me to spread the news of His love. He has sent me to let you know that you have the chance to know Him personally as a close friend, a dear father, a big brother, and an eternal helper. You might think this message isn't for you because you're already saved, but hear me out. Just like giving your life to Christ is a choice you make in your own free will, growing a deeper, more intimate relationship with him is also something you have to choose. If you believe you are as close to him as you can get, then maybe you're further away than you think.

The Gospel is the eternal Word of God that can never change. It had the power to save me at ten years old, when it was just an abstract concept in my mind. It was this same Gospel that remained planted deep in my heart when the lies of the enemy tried to bury me. The Gospel gave me the hope of light when all I saw around me was the darkness of shame, depression, and anxiety. The Gospel of Jesus anchored me to Truth even when my whole life had been shaped by lies about God, myself, and other people. The Gospel changed everything—it became my everything— but that process didn't happen overnight. In fact, it's still happening right now. Although Jesus has ultimately saved me, there is a process of sanctification in my mind, body, and spirit. This comes from walking out the Gospel, in intimate relationship with God, and it has finally allowed me to live freely.

Intimacy is a state of being deeply known and deeply loved. It is a God-given desire that each person has; however, there are various ways to fill that longing. Many people think of intimacy in the context of romantic partnerships or sex, but all healthy relationships in life— from family to friends—involve some form of intimacy. We were designed for an intimate relationship with our Creator. Before the fall, Adam and Eve lived in a perfectly intimate relationship with God. Sin came into the world and caused a separation that severed our intimacy with the Father.

The entire Bible points to the Truth of the Gospel because it is the story of God's epic plan to restore relationships with His children. Therefore, Jesus is the answer to a question that has plagued the world since the beginning of time. How can a fallen humanity be reconciled back to intimate relationship with a holy God? Jesus' crucifixion was intended not only to save your soul in death, but also to know that soul in life. Imagine the significance of that sacrifice. God thought the chance to get to know you was so valuable that He was willing to risk it all and choose you first just so that, 2,000 years later, you could possibly decide to choose Him back. And yet we walk around acting like we're doing God a favor by agreeing to follow a few of His rules. We have it backwards, yet God doesn't reject us or take back His offer of salvation and intimate relationship. He doesn't use His power to belittle us or manipulate us into serving Him. God is so good that He lets us choose, and even when we choose everything but Him, He loves us anyway.

Revelation 3:20 (NLT) says, "Look! I stand at the door and knock. If you hear my voice and open the door, I will come in, and we will share a meal together as friends." He's ready when you are, but He wants all of you, not just the parts that are easy to give. Because God is perfect, He loves us perfectly. He cares about the intimate details of our lives. We were made in His image, so our desire for intimate relationship comes from His desire for intimate relationship. However, we have free will, so God will not force us to be close to Him. He knows that forced love is not love at all.

Intimacy with God will not happen unless you seek Him deeply and intentionally. As you draw close to Him, you will be sanctified in His presence and He will draw nearer to you. He sees you through the lens of Jesus, so you cannot work to earn your salvation, but you can work to grow closer to the one who saved you. Like many Christians, I used to think relationship was a natural byproduct of salvation. I thought that the longer you belonged to Jesus, the closer you'd get to him, but that isn't the case at all. You can sit beside the same person in church, school, or work for years and never have more than a surface-level relationship with them. *Proximity does not automatically breed intimacy.* If two friends are not interested in or intentional about sharing the kind of conversations and experiences that deepen a relationship, then it will never progress. Even if you just happen to find yourself unintentionally growing close to someone, in order to maintain the same level of interaction through the various seasons of life, there needs to be a deliberate effort on both sides.

Our relationship with God works the same way. God has done a majority of the work. He already knows you and loves you perfectly. Receiving salvation requires nothing of you except belief, but if your journey with God stops there and doesn't continue on to intimate relationship, then you've missed the point of salvation entirely. If you think you're in such perfect intimacy with God that you can't go deeper, or you can't experience more, then perhaps your understanding of God needs to be expanded.

In Ephesians 3:17-19, Paul says:

Then, by constantly using your faith, the life of Christ will be released deep inside you, and the resting place of his love will become the very source and root of your life. Then you will be empowered to discover what every holy one experiences—the great magnitude of the astonishing love of Christ in all its dimensions. How deeply intimate and far-reaching is his love! How enduring and inclusive it is! Endless love beyond measurement that transcends our understanding—this extravagant love pours into you until you are filled to overflowing with the fullness of God! Never doubt God's mighty power to work in you and accomplish all this.

We must understand that an intimate, sanctifying relationship with God goes past the prayer of salvation and into living a life where we are submitted to His will. It requires deliberate communication and obedience to His commands. It requires the intentional practice of faith that roots us in God's love and fills us with His Holy Spirit. It requires allowing God to be the Savior of our souls and the Lord of our lives. We often don't see this distinction emphasized, but it is important to realize that salvation and relationship are two sides of the same coin.

It is much easier to fall into disbelief without a relationship with God. Belief isn't just what you say. It isn't just what you know in your mind. ***Belief in Jesus Christ is a heart posture that changes the way you live.*** True belief impacts your mind, body, spirit, and soul. But it is impossible to have a sustainable, lasting belief without a healthy and thriving relationship with God. Let me emphasize this by restating it a little differently. ***Knowledge is not belief.*** If your knowledge that Jesus Christ is the Son of God who died to save you from sin and death doesn't have a material impact on the way you live your life and treat others, then it is not a belief, it is just a nice idea. Your beliefs change you.

When we believe in Jesus Christ, we are saved by grace through faith (Ephesians 2:8). So it is not our actions that save us, but it is salvation that should cause us to act differently. James 2:14-20 (NLT) states:

What good is it, dear brothers and sisters, if you say you have faith but don't show it by your actions? Can that kind of faith save anyone? Suppose you see a brother or sister who has no food or clothing, and you say, "Goodbye and have a good day; stay warm and eat well"—but then you don't give that person any food or clothing. What good does that do? So you see, faith by itself isn't enough. Unless it produces good deeds, it is dead and useless. Now someone may argue, "Some people have faith; others have good deeds." But I say, "How can you show me your faith if you don't have good deeds? I will show you my faith by my good deeds." You say you have faith, for you believe that there is one God. Good for you! Even the demons believe this, and they tremble in terror. How foolish! Can't you see that faith without good deeds is useless?

So, what we come to find is that if belief is a heart posture that changes how you live through faith in Jesus Christ, and salvation requires belief, then true salvation is more than the intellectual acceptance of a theory about Christ—it is the process of faith by which God changes your heart posture in order to change your life and save your life. True faith will result in action the way that a real fruit tree must produce fruit. Jesus is a holistic savior. He will not change your heart and mind without allowing your actions to follow suit. In the words of Martin Luther, "We are saved by faith alone, but the faith that saves is never alone."[14]

---

[14] Quote by Martin Luther: 'We Are Saved by Faith Alone, but the Faith That...'" *Goodreads*, https://www.goodreads.com/quotes/26222-we-are-saved-by-faith-alone-but-the-faith-that. Accessed 1 May 2021.

...

In my life, I had many trying times that led me to grow closer to God because I used Him to feel better. However, deeper intimacy didn't develop until I made room for God to use me. It was only then that I started to actually *become* better by the power of the Holy Spirit. I am still on this journey of becoming.

While writing this book, God took me through a process of discovering deep intimacy with Him that changed my life forever. He took me to the point of no return, where I was forced to face my past and my pain and decide whether I was going to treat the symptoms of my brokenness forever or if I was finally going to deal with the disease and heal. I call this place of healing and truth the Light Point, because it exposed all the beautiful imperfections of my life under the radiance of God's glory. It was the best and scariest position I've ever been in, because I was forced entirely outside of my comfort zone. It was a space that was so frightening and unfamiliar, and yet, full of so much hope.

This period of growing closer to Christ wasn't the point I became a Christian. I am not saying that you have to have a specific level of intimacy or relationship with God in order to call yourself a follower of Christ. Once again, salvation is free. I am simply suggesting that if you are really going to "...work out your salvation with fear and trembling," as the Bible tells us to do in Philippians 2:12 (NIV), then where you start in faith cannot be where you stop.

For years, I did so much back and forth with the authenticity of my faith that my spiritual relationship with God was lukewarm at best. I had built up a house of comfort that allowed me to feel the presence of God like soft, early morning rays of sunshine beaming in through the windows, but because I was so sheltered in that house, I never knew what it felt like to stand in the direct sunlight of God's glory. The house of my comfort zone was built with fear, shame, insecurity, and people-pleasing. But when I began to seek Christ in a deep and sacrificial way, I realized that the house I'd built to protect myself was really keeping me trapped inside while blocking God out. I'd been trying to stuff Him inside a box for years, desperate to make God come to me so I wouldn't have to leave my comfort zone to go to Him. But such a small space simply couldn't contain an infinite God, so I only managed to experience bits and pieces of Him at a time.

For all those years, I knew something was missing. I knew I could go deeper, that God wanted me closer, but I loved my comfort zone. It was so nice there! I could tolerate my pain and I had a grip on my depression. I even managed to use my loneliness and anxiety to become a high achiever, both academically and socially. I'd created my own sort of false peace and happiness in the confines of my comfort zone. But when the paint began to chip and the walls began crumbling, when the beautiful exterior of the protective palace I'd built for my fear began to fade, my comfort zone started to feel suffocating rather than empowering, like a prison instead of a home. I knew I needed more of God, but it wasn't until my desire to know God overwhelmed my desire to play it safe that I allowed myself to open the doors and step out into the marvelous light of Jesus Christ.

During this time of stepping out, God led me to study Psalm 139:23-24 (NLT) which says: "Search me, O God, and know my heart; test me and know my anxious thoughts. Point out anything in me that offends you, and lead me along the path of everlasting life."

What we must realize is that intimacy with anyone, but especially with God, requires us to hold up a mirror in which we can more accurately see ourselves. It reveals things about us that we may not have seen before. When we get in God's presence through prayer, fasting, worshiping, and serving His people, we begin to see Him more clearly. When we draw near to God in this way, we begin to understand His character. It is only by holding ourselves up to His standard of perfection that we can see just how flawed and wicked we really are.

When the psalmist asked God to search his heart and know his anxious thoughts, it wasn't because God was somehow unaware of what was there. Psalm 139 is saying that when we intentionally invite God's presence to reveal to us what He already knows about us, the intimacy of that experience is humbling enough to change our hearts.

When I drew nearer to God and intentionally pursued intimacy with Him, all those areas that seemed okay in the shadowy room of my comfort zone were suddenly illuminated in the presence of the Son. I was finally in a place where significant change could occur because I saw my God and myself for who we really are. It is only when we see ourselves clearly that we can choose to change for the better. And it is a choice. Our lives are never completely still. Even if we don't realize it, we're constantly being moved in one direction or another. You can't choose what happens to you, but you can choose how you respond. Growing closer to Christ is a choice, and if you refuse to choose, then regression is the default.

The most dangerous thing, however, is to be trapped in such a dark and warped perspective that you think you are moving forward when you're actually going backward. If you don't intentionally choose to live in the light, you will unintentionally find yourself in darkness. The whole world can fall to pieces around you. A year like 2020 can turn everything you thought you knew on its head. But those who still managed to change for the better were those who were able to clearly see themselves at their worst and use what they found at that low point to grow.

God is not a genie, and choosing to follow Christ does not automatically make you better than anyone else. Yes, the Spirit of God works in you, giving you access to the power of the one true God, but you still have to make a choice to accept that power and decide to live a life of holiness. Intimacy with God doesn't necessarily make it easier to follow God; it just reveals the necessity of it. God never stops holding up the mirror for us to really see ourselves, but the problem with a lot of us is that we can't get close enough to look at it because we have gotten way too relaxed in our comfort zones. We are in proximity to the glory of God, but because we've built up walls in an effort to protect ourselves, the light of Christ can only partially reach us. In the low lighting of our comfort zones, we are constantly confronted by shadows that distort the reality of our sins, making us think we are better than we really are.

I am here to let you know that it is time to step outside. It is time to step out of your comfort zone and into the full presence of God's light. Only there can we really see ourselves for all the good, bad, and ugly. It is only there where we can become whole.

Stepping into such brightness can be a scary process because it requires immense vulnerability. Facing your inadequacy takes a massive amount of humility and courage; making the decision to do something about it takes even more. But the beautiful thing about faith is that you don't have to have everything figured out to step into the presence of God. When you choose God, you realize that He has already chosen you. When you come into His light, you are free to fall down and fall apart. You are free to release the full extent of your pain. You are free to be as broken as you really are. You don't have to hide anymore, not even from yourself, because you are ultimately seen and infinitely loved by the only one who can make you whole again. Isn't it better to fall to pieces in the hand of your Savior than to stay standing and suffering because you don't know if anyone will catch you before you hit the ground?

The devil's greatest joy would be to have a generation of almost-Christians—people who almost surrender their whole lives to God and almost see the depths of their sins. People who almost walk in the purpose of God because they almost believe He's enough for them. There is nothing that the enemy would like more than for you to be perpetually near God, but never fully *in* God because you don't realize that leaving the comfort zone is not the scariest thing. The scariest thing is to be stuck in a life of half-truth, unable to live out the purpose you were created for and incapable of walking in the destiny that God died for.

Oftentimes, we're so scared because we feel like we have to go through change alone. We're afraid of what we will find or have to give up if we are really honest with ourselves. We are afraid to admit that we love the blessings of God more than God Himself. We don't realize that there is a divine grace from Jesus Christ that gives us hope when all we can see in the mirror is defeat. There is no condemnation for those who belong to Christ Jesus. However, there is a difference between feeling condemned and being condemned. You are not condemned; that is a fact. But the devil loves to use feelings to distort facts until you believe what you feel over what is real. That's where the Holy Spirit comes in to renew our souls—our minds, wills, and emotions—so we can believe the Truth of God's love with our entire beings and seek intimacy with Him.

There is no condemnation in Jesus Christ (Romans 8:1). Not because we don't deserve condemnation, but because Christ's blood has redeemed us from our sins and we are literally made new in him. When God looks at us, He doesn't see the wretched realities of our lives. When He looks at us, God sees His beautiful children through the lens of Jesus Christ (Romans 6). Should we continue to live as if we are blissfully ignorant of eternal realities just because something feels good at the moment? No! The way God sees us should motivate us to live up to the standard He set for us.

Once you can properly see the mess of sin that Jesus took on when he died, you can better appreciate the magnitude of his sacrifice and can live in response to the love and grace that was given to you first. When you step into the light and find intimacy with God, you do not change because God loves you more, you change because you want to learn how to love Him more. You don't change because you want to get into Heaven; you could never be good enough to earn your way there. You allow the Holy Spirit to change you because you have found the most important relationship of your life and you don't want to jeopardize it. You don't want to break God's heart because, in the light, you realize that He is the definition of goodness. And through intimacy, you experience the joy of His salvation. It is the choice *to* change that makes you realize you *can't* change in your own power. However, when you make the decision to step out in faith through action, the Holy Spirit begins to do a work in you.

In the words of C.S. Lewis:

To have Faith in Christ means, of course, trying to do all that He [God] says. There would be no sense in saying you trusted a person if you would not take his advice. Thus if you have really handed yourself over to Him, it must follow that you are trying to obey Him. But trying in a new way, a less worried way. Not doing these things in order to be saved, but because He has begun to save you already. Not hoping to get to Heaven as a reward for your actions, but inevitably wanting to act in a certain way because a first faint gleam of Heaven is already inside you.[15]

Intimacy is not accidental. It is a process of relationship-building and sanctification that you enter into intentionally. God took me through the process before He revealed its

---

[15] Lewis, C.S. *Mere Christianity*. HarperOne, 2015.

significance in my life. In hindsight, however, He has called me simply to explain something that was so confusing and painful for me. God wants intimacy with you, and as you see God, know God, and love God, you can experience His intimate Gospel too.

An Intimate Gospel

Nine

RISE AND SHINE

God mastered all my broken pieces
Using the shattered shards of my reality to create
His masterpiece
In my weakness, His might was magnified
Grace illuminated
Out of hiding, bought with a price
I am Redeemed
Set Free by Christ I point to the light,
Daring you to stare directly at the Son
of God.

hen we choose life in the light, we become living, breathing expressions of God's love. Living in the light means realizing that you don't shine for yourself. You are simply a beacon of hope poured out for others and constantly recharged by the love of God. Matthew 5:14-16 (NIV) says:

> You are the light of the world. A town built on a hill cannot be hidden. Neither do people light a lamp and put it under a bowl. Instead they put it on its stand, and it gives light to everyone in the house. In the same way, let your light shine before others, that they may see your good deeds and glorify your Father in heaven.

We should never be afraid to shine because we are not representing ourselves. Our lives only shine to point to the light of our Father in Heaven. The irony is that being the light of the world means that your life isn't about you, but at the same time, it requires all of you. When we are born again, we share in the death and life of Christ. We become one Body unified in him; but I must let you know that your specific story matters. Everything that you are and everything that you've been through can be used in the light. When the reality of your life meets the Truth of God's Word, you are able to shine like no one else.

Understanding that we are the light of the world is a call to self-love and unity at the same time. I am united with my brothers and sisters in the Body of Christ because each of us is a point of light that points to the Truth of the Gospel.

We exist for God's glory, not our own. However, I am also called to celebrate the unique testimony that God has given me because the way He created me was intentional. His plans for my life are specific and He loves all of me, even those parts that are still in the dark. Light exposes the lies and reveals the Truth.

We often talk about speaking our truths, and while being authentic is important, sometimes we can get so caught up in who we are that we forget who we were created to be. Sometimes we can focus so much on our truths that we never see *the* Truth. The Light Point is a place in the presence of God where we are set free from the confines of the narratives we've created for ourselves and live boldly in the knowledge that our lives are less about us and more about the kingdom of God. Living in the light means seeing God, knowing God, and loving God every day. It is the point at which you stop shining for yourself by trying to outshine others. It is the moment you understand that only when you reach the end of yourself can you shine as brightly as God has called you to.

If you are living in the light, people will see you. They might clap for you, but they will ultimately praise your God because you are not the point of all of this; He is. But, my dear friend, if you are living in the darkness or you are unsure because your life moves in and out of faith like shifting shadows, please be encouraged. If you carry shame or fear, if you wear depression like a heavy weight, if you are incapacitated by insecurity or pain, I have to let you know that the light of the Gospel changes everything. It may not bring you out of the darkness this very second, but it is more than able to bring the darkness out of you.

The light does not judge you—it gives you hope. You have access to the answer, so freedom is much closer than it feels. God doesn't run away from your darkness; He draws closer. Light isn't made to shine where it's already bright, it was made to shine where it is needed—in the dark. If you seek Him, He will find you, because no matter how dark the night, you can always look forward to joy in the morning sun.

> *For his anger lasts only a moment,*
> *but his favor lasts a lifetime!*
> *Weeping may last through the night,*
> *but joy comes with the morning.*

Psalms 30:5 (NLT)

...

I wrote this book because my struggle isn't just for me. My ability to stop and get insight on what I've gone through and learn from the ugliest parts of myself is not an accident. It is a gift that God has divinely placed in my hand to help His people get free. This freedom is not mystical; it is divine. It will not happen overnight, but there is a repeatable process that you can follow. I've seen first-hand how it transformed me from a sexually immoral, insecure, selfish, prideful person into someone who isn't completely fixed, but who is completely free. Let me keep it real. I still struggle...a lot! I still deal with insecurity, anxiety, and fear in some ways. I fall, fail, and falter. Even with all the revelation that God has given me to write this book, sometimes I still find myself in sin daily. I battle lust, pride, and unforgiveness. The only difference is grace. By the grace of God, overcoming doesn't mean that I never deal with the things God has freed me from. It just means that they no longer have power over me. Because I now know the truth, I already have the victory. I don't have to struggle because I have surrendered. This way of learning to see God, know God, and love God has brought me out of the darkness and into the wonderful light.

I am someone who genuinely appeared to have it all together, when all the while, I was breaking on the inside. Little did I know that God would build something beautiful out of those broken-down walls. It's very obvious now that I don't have all the answers, but in the space of vulnerability, God made me whole. He helped me so I could point others back to His light, back to the place of healing. I typed the words, but this story was written by the Holy Spirit. I hope his presence in these pages has brought you a little bit closer to the Light Point.

It is important for me to release this book now, while I am still young and largely unaccomplished, for several reasons. The primary reason is to ensure only God gets the glory. The Bible says:

Remember, dear brothers and sisters, that few of you were wise in the world's eyes or powerful or wealthy when God called you. Instead, God chose things the world considers foolish in order to shame those who think they are wise. And he chose things that are powerless to shame those who are powerful. God chose things despised by the world, things counted as nothing at all, and used them to bring to nothing what the world considers important. As a result, no one can ever boast in the presence of God (1 Corinthians 1:26-29 NIV).

As I contemplate this verse, I think of all the reasons I didn't believe I was in a position to write this book. I am not influential or well-known. I have yet to accomplish many things that would be considered wise or strong or impressive in the eyes of the world. But none of those are criteria for being called, and I have been called.

Although we read this scripture, we still want to find an example of someone in proximity to us who has been called in the same manner, someone for whom answering the call worked out well. I always want to find a review or a YouTube demo for everything, but there is no unboxing video for my calling. There is no way of knowing exactly how it will turn out. That's why it takes faith.

We hear this verse quoted a lot when people are trying to be humble or explain to us that anyone can be called. But the irony of it is that we often hear this verse quoted by people during times in their lives when the world wouldn't necessarily find them foolish at all. We hear it from people who have achieved some level of success in their career or family or ministry. We often hear this verse from people who are looking way back on their foolishness.

Although God called them at a time when they were inadequate, in a way, their testimonies gain validity because at the time they speak out, their lives look impressive. They might still be in the growing process, as we all are, but for the most part, we hear this verse from people who have come all the way out of what they went through. I think that in many ways, this is very wise. They are far enough from their experiences to reflect on them and teach us what they learned. That's what I initially wanted. I didn't want to publish my pain while I was still processing it. I didn't want to allow others to see me until I could fully look at myself.

For so long, I wondered why God insisted that I write now, speak out now, testify now. Wouldn't my testimony be so much more beautiful and inspiring coming from a greater vantage point, at a time when I could stand further from my brokenness and closer to restoration? I thank God that I am no longer in the dark, but in some ways, I thought I should get the chance to experience the light for a little while longer before I told the whole world to join me there.

I think it takes a different kind of grace to testify in the anticipation of complete healing than it does to testify in the memory of it. The grace is not better or greater, it is simply different. In a way, writing this testimony now draws you, the reader, into my process of having faith for what God will ultimately do with all my broken pieces. He has made me whole, but my store is far from finished. In fact, it has only just begun. So writing this book now invites you to hope with me, grow with me, and trust with me. I hope this book will help you understand that if we attempt to let the light in only when we think we're finished forming, we might find that the illuminated version of ourselves is unrecognizable. We may realize that because we attempted to get clean in the dark, we are forced to address the areas we missed under a much greater spotlight than we ever anticipated.

To put it plainly, for me, this book is an act of obedience. I believe God needed me to release it now, before I made a name for myself, because there were parts of my recovery that simply required more light, the kind of light that comes from radical transparency, the kind of light that comes in the blessing of being able to process your pain enough to make something beautiful out of it. There is a level of vulnerability, freedom from the fear of man, and complete surrender to God that could only have come from writing and publishing this book here and now, before I have any accolades or accomplishments to lean on for validation. In this moment, God has to be enough, because He's all I have.

God doesn't just use the foolish things of this world to confuse the wise after they've stopped appearing foolish. He uses those things right there, in the midst of their foolishness. If we will allow ourselves to be called by a God who sees us how He created us to be, instead of how we currently are, then we give God permission to set us free.

The Bible says that we overcome by the blood of the lamb and the word of our testimony (Revelation 12:11). The blood was already shed for my sins, so now all I have left to give is my testimony. The Bible didn't say we are saved by the blood and the testimony. It is the blood, and the blood alone, that gives us the gift of salvation. However, we find that overcoming doesn't automatically come in a nicely wrapped package alongside salvation. Since the blood was already shed, the overcoming happens whenever you decide to testify. And the overcoming may never happen if you remain silent.

All too often, we equate overcoming with achieving a certain level of success. We say that when we have a healthy family we will have overcome our toxic perspective of relationships, or when we graduate we will have overcome all the academic and financial obstacles that stood in our way. However, we must be careful not to conflate overcoming in the physical with overcoming in the spiritual. Revelation 12:11 is speaking of a supernatural overcoming. It is the kind of overcoming that happens when you let the light of God's Truth shine on your experience. It is a spiritual process, and it isn't anchored in any physical timelines or benchmarks. It simply happens when you let the light in.

When you choose to speak, when you refuse to let what you have been through define you, when you share your story, when you allow the work God has done in you to go far beyond yourself so other people can be transformed by the light of Christ, that is when you overcome. None of our stories happen in a vacuum; therefore, none of our testimonies happen in isolation. God didn't just come to save my body, He came to save the Body. The Body of Christ. My overcoming, my joy, and my faith can never be complete unless it is rooted in love for God and my brothers and sisters in the faith. That is why I cannot be silent. There is someone whose testimony is connected to my testimony. There is someone whose breakthrough is directly correlated with my obedience.

While it may feel good to live freely and in purpose, our ultimate goal is not just to be happy; it is to live in a way that exalts our Heavenly Father. So as hard as it has been, I can overcome right here, right now, at twenty-three— even though I'm still a bit scared and looking at a long journey ahead to wholeness. I can overcome, I have overcome, and I am overcoming in the mighty name of Jesus. You can, too, at any age. It is never too early and it is never too late. This book is the evidence of that. If I can do it, then what's stopping you?

So I pray for you, dear reader. I pray that you hear my story and praise God. I pray that you choose, this day and every day after, to live in the Light Point.

About the Author

Siji's full name is Oluwasijibomi, and she hails proudly from Nigeria. She is a graduate of the University of Texas at Austin and is a resident of Dallas, Texas. She currently works as a business consultant and serves as a church youth teacher at Redeem Christian Church of God House on the Rock Parish.

As a Nigerian American, logically creative thinker, frugal shopaholic, talkative introvert, and feminist Christian, Siji is someone who has always been defined by duality. She is a young woman on a mission to point people to their identities in Christ in a world that, for too long, tried to define her based on what she did rather than who she was.

Siji has a blog that is also called The Light Point. Through vulnerability and transparency, she uses her platform to share her story and amplify the stories of others. Her mission is to share content that encourages others, motivates better questions, and ultimately points to the light of Christ.

You can find more of Siji's content, as well as her blog, at sijideleawe.com.

Made in the USA
Columbia, SC
16 June 2021

40042098R00117